Reopen With Confidence

A GUIDE FOR RESTAURANTS IN THE COVID-19 ERA

Deveoped by Merril Gilbert and Rhiannon Woo

ISBN 978-1-7352096-1-6 (paperback)

ISBN 978-1-7352096-0-9 (e-book)

Published by MMR Specialty Foods, LLC

About the Authors

Merril Gilbert

CEO and Co-founder MMR Specialty Foods

The catalyst of creative development and investment for everything food and beverage, Merril leverages 25 years of experience to guide companies from development to launch of innovative new products, establish brand identity, and grow categories. Always at the forefront of emerging trends on the future of food, technology, food safety, health and wellness, the recent expansion of legal Cannabis is the next frontier to scale.

in www.linkedin.com/in/merril-gilbert/

Rhiannon Woo

CSO and Co-founder MMR Specialty Foods

Rhiannon is a sought-out leader in Food Safety development and protocol. An expert in Good Agricultural Practices, Good Harvesting Practices, Good Manufacturing Practices, HACCP, and the Food Safety Modernization Act, since 2007. Her distinctive background in food and beverage manufacturing makes her an ideal partner for companies striving to produce the highest quality, most reliable products.

in www.linkedin.com/in/rhiannon-woo/

We want to thank Laurine Wickett of Left Coast Catering and Henry Dombey, Clubsoda Productions for providing our cover photo.

Table of Contents

Introduction

The opportunity to re-open dine-in restaurants, bars, breweries, and wineries after months of disrupted business is appreciated and daunting. These types of businesses are hands on operations that will require rethinking every aspect of your daily service procedures. Employees and the public want assurances that owners and managers can demonstrate their commitment to their well-being and safety.

For the vast majority of operators there are a variety of downloadable guidelines from the CDC and individual states providing basic and broad directives for public safety. This book goes deeper with step-by-step details to make the process more effective for employees and customers to build a higher level of trust and confidence in your business practices.

Providing a safe environment for employees and customers is important to rebuild trust. There is no one way fits all and each type of business will require its own plan. This book provides companies a written worksite-specific COVID-19 reopening plan that can be adapted for each location.

This book can be used to develop your written documentation to meet state and local requirements which should be available on-site at each location.

Background

In early March of 2020 the spread of COVID-19 began to unfold quickly and by April 2020 almost all businesses were forced to temporarily close down. The restaurant, hospitality, retail and travel sectors were immediately impacted with the majority ceasing all operations.

By mid-May 2020 many states have eased their restrictions and once again allowing some business to re-open with modified operating guidelines. It is not an easy task to just open the doors, it requires careful consideration that must include everything from financial implications, new training, sanitation, menu, communications, and re-configurations of dining and public access areas. This book removes the guesswork and includes worksheets and checklists to make sure nothing is overlooked.

We are stronger together and here to assist.

Merril & Rhiannon
MMR Specialty Foods

Disclaimer

The information provided in this book does not, and is not intended to, constitute legal advice; instead, all information, content, and materials available in this book and supplemental references are for general informational purposes only. Information in this book may not constitute the most up-to-date legal or other information. This book and supplemental resources contain links to other third-party websites, and documents. Such links are only for the convenience of the reader or user; MMR Specialty Foods, LLC and its associates do not recommend or endorse the contents of the third-party sites or reference materials. In addition, the publisher and the authors assume no responsibility for errors, inaccuracies, omissions, or any other inconsistencies herein.

Readers of this book should contact their attorney to obtain advice with respect to any particular legal matter. Only your individual attorney can provide assurances that the information contained herein – and your interpretation of it – is applicable or appropriate to your particular business or situation. Use of, and access to, this book or any of the links or resources contained within the book does not create an attorney-client relationship between the reader or user and authors and contributors, or their respective employers.

While our guidance notes general employee and operational considerations, the actual impact of the relevant employer actions and procedures will vary from employer to employer and based on the specific actions taken and in accordance with national, state, county, and city guidelines and regulations. We suggest that companies and employers seek legal counsel with respect to employee and customer related implications of specific employment and/or public safety actions regarding potential liabilities.

The views expressed at, or through, this book are those of the individual authors writing in their individual capacities only as a whole. All liability with respect to actions taken or not taken based on the contents of this book is hereby expressly disclaimed. The content herein is provided "as is;" no representations are made that the content is error-free.

1

Financial Considerations

Financial Operations Overview

Reopening businesses safely for employees and customers requires planning, training, and communication. Deciding to re-open now or remain closed until later in the year takes careful consideration. The restaurant and foodservice industry generally runs on very low profit margins. It is important to take the time to evaluate if reopening with a modified and limited service model is right for your company.

* The COVID-19 pandemic situation is changing almost daily in regards to laws, regulations and guidelines. This book provides guidance specific to reopening a food and beverage business and may not reflect the most recent national, state, and local announcements.

Before constructing barriers, moving tables, and stocking up on disinfectant it is important to answer the following questions:

I. What local health and safety requirements orders are required for reopening?
   A. Review reopening guidelines for your city, county, and state
      1. State Department of Public Health (DPH)
      2. City – Department of Public Health
      3. Centers for Disease Control and Prevention (CDC)
      4. OSHA
      5. U.S. Food and Drug Administration (FDA)
II. Has the business received Paycheck Protection Program (PPP) and/or Grant Funds?
   A. Do these funds and loans give the business enough runway to remain closed or offer modified services for up to 6 months?
   B. Review with Bank and Accountant to fully understand the forgiveness or payback requirements
III. What are the financial considerations for reopening?

A. Revenue projections based on limited service
   1. Reduced hours of operation
   2. On-site pickup and take-out plus third-party delivery service fees
   3. 25 -50% less seating
   4. Slower table turns to allow for sanitizing between each seating
   5. Fewer menu offerings
   6. Variance in cost of goods sold (COGs)
      a. Increase to operating expenses
      b. Disruptions to supply chain
   7. Build projections based on
      a. Each day of the week
      b. Reduced hours of operations
      c. Number of orders for take-out vs. dine-in
      d. Estimated check average with revised menu
   8. Projected labor costs
      a. How many employees needed for each shift
      b. Staggered schedules
      c. Restricted operating hours and/or days per week

IV. What will it cost to modify operations to re-open?
   A. Conduct a comprehensive walk through of entire business location to identify all human contact touch points to assess risk and adjustments for employee and customer use. (This topic is also covered in Section 3 - Creating Your C-19 Prevention Plan)
   B. Start at front entrance – exterior & interior
      1. Doors, windows, gates
      2. Outside seating
      3. Window coverings
      4. Identify high touch surfaces (examples)
         a. Door handles
         b. Equipment
         c. POS systems
         d. Trash
         e. Items that should no longer be shared
            i. Pens

ii. Clipboards

iii. Utensils – sanitize between use

5. Host station – how much direct contact with guests?

   a. Menu storage

   b. Menu style

      i. Should be paper and disposable or posted electronically where guest does not touch or handle

6. Quick serve – counter ordering and payment

   a. Can the space be divided with one side order placement and one side pickup?

   b. Define where people wait for orders or wait for table

   c. If dining in – how to limit where people can sit

   d. Alternatives to self-serve condiments and beverages

      i. Beverage vendor may need to exchange self serve station to behind counter – space and plumbing considerations

7. Dining room and service stations

   a. Tables, chairs, booths – how close are they to each other

      i. Modifications for social distancing

      ii. Limiting number of customers at a table

   b. Trash areas

   c. Storage of flatware, condiments, paper goods, napkins

   d. POS – point of sale – is it a touchscreen

      i. Cash handling – can you go cashless

      ii. Daily bookkeeping and deposits

      iii. Credit card processing

      iv. Is it used as a time clock for employees to sign in and out

8. Bar area

   a. Behind bar work areas

   b. Bottles and storage

   c. Refrigeration

   d. Glass washing

   e. Storage areas

   f. Equipment, utensils and storage containers

   g. Trash

        h.   Service bar

   9. Storage areas – front of the house

  10. Kitchen

        a.   Storage areas

        b.   Walk-ins and freezers

        c.   Cook line

            i.   Hoods

           ii.   Ovens

          iii.   Grills

          iv.   Stovetop

            v.   Induction cooktops

        d.   Prep areas

        e.   Dishwashing and cleaning storage

        f.   Hand washing sinks

        g.   Equipment and utensils

        h.   Laundry and linen clean and soiled placement

  11. Restrooms and employee areas

        a.   Deep cleaning ahead of reopening

        b.   Implementing hourly cleaning and sanitizing schedule for public restrooms

        c.   Space for employees to store personal items and change of clothes

            i.   Needs to cleaned and sanitized between each shift

  12. Exterior

        a.   Trash receptacles and pickup schedule

        b.   Receiving

        c.   Cleaning and maintenance

C. Reconfiguring dining/bar areas, kitchen workspaces, storage to facilitate safe distancing, sanitation, and ability to wash hands and/or sanitize

D. Construction costs as needed

   1. Barriers and partitions to create separation

   2. Additional areas for hand washing and sanitizing

E. Labor costs for training

F. Purchasing personal protective equipment (PPE) for employees and customers

G. Cleaning services and supplies

H. Daily health and temperature screenings
   1. Recommended for all employees and managers
   2. Recommended for customers and visitors to business
I. Implementing a reservation system to space guest seating
J. Working with neighborhood to create outdoor seating
K. Printing expenses
   1. Menus
   2. Signage

V. Changes to services offered
   A. Limiting menu
      1. Allows for fewer employees on site
      2. Limits actual dining time by guests at a table
         a. Less exposure to employees and other guests
      3. Offset potential increases to product costs
      4. Lower inventory = more cash flow
      5. Supply chain – what is available without disruption?
      6. Staggering and/or less deliveries, avoiding any drop offs inside location if possible
      7. Focuses on what business is known for
      8. Ability to execute for dine-in and take-out
         a. Packaging for take-out
         b. Tabletop – disposable or china, glass, and silverware?
            i. Condiments – individually packaged
            ii. Utensils, cups, plates, glassware
            iii. Napkins
               · Higher quality paper to wrap silverware
            iv. Place for Guests to safely place mask while eating
            v. Is hand sanitizer on table or individual wipes provided to each guest upon being seated?
         c. Sanitizing all surfaces throughout day
            i. Restrooms
            ii. Between each guest seating
   B. Define daily hours of operation
      1. Are there local or state restrictions on hours of operation?

2. Base operating hours on type of menu being offer
3. Types of service – dine-in and take-out or just one or the other
4. Aligning with third-party delivery services
    a. Look at service agreement – can fees be negotiated lower?
5. Staffing and scheduling
    a. Can schedule be staggered for less contact between staff members
    b. Define each area where employees will work and how many required to execute menu
        i. Dining room
        ii. Bar
        iii. Kitchen
        iv. Receiving – try to have all products dropped outside limiting number of people who enter building
        v. Take out – prep, packing and pickup
C. The alternative dining experiences
    1. Seating directly at bar may not be feasible for physical distancing
        a. Can a partition be place between bartender and customers?
    2. Blocking tables or placing partitions between tables to maintain physical separation
    3. Separated area for pickup of take-out/delivery orders
    4. Exterior signage and floor markings to communicate social distancing
    5. Customers not waiting at entrance to be seated
        a. Reservations recommended to control flow and avoid congested wait areas
        b. Customers should wear masks upon entering and departing – **This is an act of kindness to protect everyone's well being**
        c. Host – wearing mask and access to hand sanitizer
    6. Is outside dining an option for your location?
    7. Ventilation
        a. Is outside air available and optimal for not creating a pest issue?
        b. Scheduling a ventilation and hood cleaning service ahead of opening
        c. If located with a multi-use building (e.g. office building) what precautions is building management implementing to ensure clean airflow?

VI.   Technology upgrades – this may be the time for new tech
   A.   As part of your business assessment look to adaptations where human contact can be alleviated
      1.   Time clocks that also take your temperature
      2.   On-line banking, accounting and HR
         a.   Online HR and Payroll services are good resources for providing updated information and guidelines for how to communicate COVID-19 sickness and leaves of absence policies.
      3.   POS – point of sale that works with cashless payments
      4.   Apps that provide a bar code that customer can use with smartphone to see menu
         a.   You can even order and pay directly from these
      5.   E-commerce – add on to website
      6.   Reservation or waitlist app that can also assist with contact tracing if needed
      7.   Robotics – is there an automated solution that you can use?
   B.   Time to negotiate
      1.   Many monthly service fees are being waived or discounted
   C.   Remember to factor all monthly service fees into your revised budgetary forecast
VII.   Return to work policies - legal, insurance and human resource (HR)
   A.   Legal
      1.   Determine if your business should or must engage in health screenings and establish clear guidelines
         a.   Type of screenings
         b.   Frequency
         c.   Reporting obligations
      2.   Understand employee privacy rights
      3.   What is required documentation and retention of health screening logs
   B.   Insurance
      1.   Connect with Insurance company on current updates and/or modifications to business, workman's comp, liability and benefits policies
   C.   HR – return to work and rehire policies
      1.   Implementing health and wellness screenings and procedures
         a.   Meet local and state requirements
         b.   All employees have current food safety training

   c. Clear defined company policy for employees prior to each shift and if employee is sick at work

   d. Set protocols for employees who test positive for COVID-19 and for those who show symptoms

      i. Include workplace contact tracing

      ii. Reporting to government agencies

      iii. Disclosing to other employees or customers

      iv. Requirements for returning to work

      v. Sanitizing workspaces and equipment that may have been used by infected employee and those employees within close proximity

2. Updates to "at will" employment policies – check with HR Specialist and/or legal council

3. Revising leave policies – Protected time off and pay may be required

   a. For employees that are ill or become ill

   b. Are the caretaker for someone in their household who is ill

   c. No access to childcare

   d. Fearful of returning to work

4. Updates to uniform – to include

   a. If PPE is required employer should supply or reimburse for costs

   b. Personal hygiene and uniform cleanliness

   c. Facemasks - covering nose, mouth, chin

   d. Proper use of gloves

   e. Storage of clothing during shift

   f. What will be provided for each shift

   g. If employee or manager arrives without PPE that is required and is not provided they can be sent home to retrieve without pay

5. Personal belongings – limiting what can be brought in

   a. Cell phone use and storage at work

   b. Sanitation of personal items and safe storage at work

6. Rehiring employees

   a. Review and manage employees on leave, furloughed, or laid off for workers compensation claims, FMLA and/or other leaves of absence

   b. Check federal, state and local unemployment insurance and CARES

Act benefits that may effect rehires and if only returning part-time.

    c.   Update paperwork electronically including ability to sign documents

    d.   Prepare response for employees who do not want to return to work – *consult HR Specialist and/or legal council for correct wording of this statement*

   7.   New hires

    a.   Interviews – recommend virtual

       i.   If in person be sure they wear facemasks

    b.   Conditional job offer

       i.   May delay start date or may withdraw job offer if not able to reasonable accommodate for later start date

    c.   Screening for COVID-19 symptoms

       i.   Is a COVID-19 test required before job offer or first day?

       ii.   Check with Legal council on who pays for test?

    d.   New hire paperwork should be electronic, including ability to sign documents.

D.   Training – leading change in actions and processes

   1.   Each area of your business will require a training process

    a.   Involve managers in developing the programs

    b.   Train the Trainers – for on-going success

    c.   Hold daily pre-shift meetings with all employees

       i.   Emphasize the new procedures

       ii.   Inform of any changes

       iii.   To check in on what is working and where to improve

VIII.   Communication and marketing

A.   Develop messaging that communicates to employees, vendors and customers how your company is addressing their safety.

B.   Look for visual ways to communicate a clean and safe environment

   1.   Signage from exterior of business and throughout location

   2.   Creative examples

    a.   Hand sanitizer on every table and in all public access areas

    b.   Individual paper bags fro guest to place facemask while eating

    c.   Having disposable masks available for customers

    d.   Many paper and cleaning suppliers have created a variety of single use options from hand sanitizer to facemasks for employees and guests

3. Social media announcements
   a. Wearing facemasks
   b. How to place orders
   c. Going cashless
   d. Reservations and waiting for tables
   e. Pickup and delivery practices
   f. Photos of employees preparing orders safely
4. Marketing – announce reopening and tell your story
   a. Instagram & Instagram Live
      i. Live kitchen prep shots with employees wearing masks
      ii. Social distancing – creative approaches
      iii. Chef's take-home kit to prepare their special dish
   b. Blogs – share your journey
   c. PR local media if doing something unique
      i. Think glass houses in Amsterdam
      ii. Dressed mannequins, cardboard outs or blowup dolls for social distancing
   d. Unique offerings
      i. With alcohol being able to be sold to go – maybe it is time to sell overstock of spirits and wine

2

Financial Worksheets

How to Create a 3-Month Reopening Operating Financial Plan

In the Financial Operations Overview we outlined each area of consideration that business owners need to address prior to reopening. In many instances the operation has either been completely closed or operating only with take-out and delivery service. All have suffered financial loss and working with limited cash flow. The worksheets presented demonstrate a three-month financial plan.

The following assumptions were used to create this model and demonstrate how to prepare one based on your operations. It should be noted that these assumptions do not reflect any financial relief that a company may have negotiated specific to their business, such as reduction or rent forbearance. It does factor in an example if the company received $50,000 from the Payroll Protection Program (PPP) or Grant.

- Sales Forecast – The base revenue model
- Labor Cost
- Reopening Expenses
- 3-Month Financial Forecast

The Sales Forecast is based on a 7-day restaurant serving three meal periods, breakfast, lunch and dinner. Operating hours from 7am to 8pm. The sales mix is 70% Food, 30% Beverage. Estimated Cost of Good Sold, is 28% Food Cost and 18% Blended Beverage Cost.

Sales Assumption Check Average:

- Breakfast - $9
- Lunch - $11
- Dinner - $20

Customer counts used for revenue forecast are moderate by meal period with slight increases on weekends.

The model does not breakdown individual operating expenses, but the four main categories:

- Labor – Company Staffing
- Marketing and Administrative
- Operating Supplies – (e.g. utilities, paper goods, cleaning supplies and equipment)
- Occupancy

Labor Model includes, 2 salaried employees with a lead cook and lead server to balance management activities. Front and Back of the House scheduling is based on a limited menu with minimal staff to facilitate scaled back operations and number of people inside the workplace.

Other Expenses are listed as 1% of sales and 1% of sales for Depreciation and Amortization.

Reopening Expenses captures estimated costs that a business may need to increase sanitation practices, materials and construction to adapt workplace for social distancing, marketing and PR to tell the story of reopening and promote business, and fees to cover additional consulting for legal and human resource advisors.

It is recommended to complete this exercise to determine if reopening can be financially sustainable with limited service for the next three months. In the example presented there is a loss even with a PPP/Grant until the third month. It will take time to rebuild business, as this is a fluid situation that is evolving daily. It is important to define what is best for your business at this point in time and what steps can be taken to manage cash flow until sales stabilize.

Sample 3 Month Operating Forecast

3-Month Operating Projections - Based on Limited Menu & Service

	Month 1	% of Sales	Month 2 (30% Increase)	%	Month 3 (60% Increase)	
Sales						
Food	$72,800	70%	$94,640	70%	$151,424	70%
Beverage	$31,200	30%	$40,560	30%	$64,896	30%
Total Sales	**$104,000**	**100%**	**$135,200**	**100%**	**$216,320**	**100%**
Cost of Sales						
Food	$29,120	28%	$37,856	28%	$60,570	28%
Beverage	$18,720	18%	$20,280	15%	$32,448	15%
Total Cost of Sales	**$47,840**	**46%**	**$58,136**	**43%**	**$93,018**	**43%**
GROSS PROFIT	**$56,160**	**54%**	**$77,064**	**57%**	**$123,302**	**57%**
Estimated Expense to Reopen						
Location & Build-out Costs	$5,000					
Marketing & PR	$1,750					
Legal + HR Consulting	$5,000		$5,000		$2,500	
Total RE-open Costs	**$11,750**	**11%**	**$5,000**	**4%**	**$2,500**	**1%**
Operating Costs						
Company Staffing	$56,550	54%	$56,550	42%	$56,550	26%
Marketing & Admin	$2,080	2%	$2,028	2%	$3,245	2%
Operating Supplies	$10,400	10%	$12,168	9%	$19,469	9%
Occupancy Costs	$5,000	5%	$5,000	4%	$5,000	2%
Total Operating Costs	**$74,030**	**71%**	**$75,746**	**56%**	**$84,264**	**39%**
Other (Income) Expense						
Other (Income) Expense	$1,040	1%	$1,352	1%	$2,163	1%
Interest Expense	$0		$0		$0	
Depreciation & Amortizati	$1,040	1%	$1,352	1%	$2,163	1%
Total Other Expense	**$2,080**	**2%**	**$2,704**	**2%**	**$4,326**	**2%**
NET INCOME BEFORE TAXES	**($40,020)**		**($25,314)**		**$1,928**	
Est. PPP - Grants	$25,000		$25,000		$0	
CASH FLOW BEFORE INCOME TAXES	**($15,020)**		**($314)**		**$1,928**	

Sample Revenue Model

Sales and Labor Assumptions

ESTIMATE OF AVERAGE CHECK BY MEAL PERIOD *

Based on Estimated Check Average of Limited Menu Offering

	MONDAY	TUESDAY	WEDNESDAY	THURSDAY	FRIDAY	SATURDAY	SUNDAY
BREAKFAST	$9	$9	$9	$9	$9	$9	$9
LUNCH	$11	$11	$11	$11	$11	$11	$11
DINNER	$20	$20	$20	$20	$20	$20	$20

ESTIMATE OF CUSTOMER COUNTS PER DAY OF THE WEEK

	MONDAY	TUESDAY	WEDNESDAY	THURSDAY	FRIDAY	SATURDAY	SUNDAY
BREAKFAST	50	50	50	50	70	85	85	440
LUNCH	75	75	75	75	90	125	125	640
DINNER	100	100	100	100	125	125	100	750

ESTIMATE OF PROSPECTIVE DAILY SALES

	MONDAY	TUESDAY	WEDNESDAY	THURSDAY	FRIDAY	SATURDAY	SUNDAY
BREAKFAST	$450	$450	$450	$450	$630	$765	$765	$3,960
LUNCH	$825	$825	$825	$825	$990	$1,375	$1,375	$7,040
DINNER	$2,000	$2,000	$2,000	$2,000	$2,500	$2,500	$2,000	$15,000

TOTAL WEEK SALES $26,000

TOTAL MONTH SALES $104,000

Sample Labor Model

Labor Plan

HOURLY STAFF

Position Description	Estimated Daily Start Time	Estimated Daily End Time	Daily Hours - minus break	Wage Rate ($/hr)	Total Daily Wages	Days Per Week	TOTAL WEEK HOURLY
Back of the House							
Utility	8am	4pm	7.5	$10.00	$75.00	7	$525
Utility	2pm	10pm	7.5	$10.00	$75.00	7	$525
Prep	6am	2pm	7.5	$12.00	$90.00	7	$630
Prep	9am	5pm	7.5	$12.00	$90.00	7	$630
Cook	7am	3pm	7.5	$14.00	$105.00	7	$735
Cook	9am	5pm	7.5	$14.00	$105.00	7	$735
Lead Cook	1pm	9pm	7.5	$19.00	$142.50	7	$998
Front of the House							
Busser	7am	3pm	7.5	$10.00	$75.00	7	$525
Busser	1pm	9pm	7.5	$10.00	$75.00	7	$525
Server	7am	3pm	7.5	$10.00	$75.00	7	$525
Server	1pm	9pm	7.5	$10.00	$75.00	7	$525
Lead Server	2pm	10pm	7.5	$15.00	$112.50	7	$788
Host	12pm	8pm	7.5	$12.00	$90.00	7	$630
				$158.00			$8,295

Fringe Rate: 38% $3,152

Total Direct Labor: $ 11,447

SALARIED STAFF

	Wage	TOTAL WEEK SALARY
Chef	$50,000	$962
Manager	$50,000	$962
	$100,000	$1,923

Fringe Rate: 40% $769

Total Salary Labor: $2,692

TOTAL PERSONNEL COST: $14,139

$56,558 COST PER MONTH

* fringe rate is benfits cost and payroll taxes

Sample Reopening Budget

Estimated Expenses for Reopening

Location Buildout	Budget	Actual	+/-
Cleaning, PPE Supplies	$2,500		
Materials + Construction	$2,500		
	$5,000		

Marketing + PR			
Printing	$250		
Promotion	$500		
PR	$1,000		
	$1,750		

Legal + HR Consulting			
Legal	$3,500		
Human Resources	$1,500		
	$5,000		

| **Total** | **$11,750** | | |

3

Create Your COVID-19 Prevention Plan

Foundation Steps

Establish a COVID-19 Prevention Plan Team

You will first need to designate your Team Leader. This is a critical role, the team leader will be responsible for ensuring the plan is developed, implemented and maintained. This should be someone within business who has authority and responsibility to make in the moment decisions, such as whether to close off a section of the dining room, cancel reservations, or remove patrons. This should also be someone who is regularly onsite during operations.

It is not likely for one person to have all the skills necessary to design an effective COVID-19 Prevention Plan. Just as running your restaurant takes different types of expertise, your COVID-19 Prevention Plan requires the input, buy-in and support of your team's front of house and back of house leadership. Assembling a team whose members have a good knowledge of the product and process is essential. The team should be able to identify hazards, determine risks, recommend controls, recommend enforcement steps and conduct research if information is not available. A well-rounded team will have members representing both back of the house staff and front of the house staff, as well as individuals who understand microbiology and regulatory requirements. It may be necessary to seek outside advice, especially during the risk assessment process. This assistance might be available from a local restaurant association or from food safety or sanitation consultants you have worked with in the past.

When choosing individuals to be on your COVID-19 Prevention Plan Team (C-19 Team), here are some things to consider:

- How well does this individual understand your products?
- How well does this individual understand your patrons?
- How well does this individual understand your team dynamics and workplace culture?
- How well does this individual understand how COVID-19 is transmitted?
- How well does this individual understand workplace safety?
- Can this individual be relied on to set a good example for the rest of the staff, when

it comes to following the plan once it is established?

It is also important to ensure that within the team there is at least working level knowledge of the following areas:

- Ingredient purchasing
- Ingredient receiving
- Dry goods and refrigerated ingredient storage
- Ingredient prep
- Kitchen management
- Dining room setup
- Patron waiting area management
- Patron service expectations
- Checkout process
- Cleaning and Janitorial

Team Leader:
Helen Young – General Manager

Team Members:
Mitchell Fernandez – Kitchen Manager
Ray Spears – Dining Room Manager
Lauren Yee – Cleaning Crew Manager

Team Experience Matrix

		Ingredient Purchasing	Ingredient Receiving	Dry Goods and Refrigerated Ingredient	Ingredient Prep	Kitchen Management	Dining Room Setup	Patron waiting area management	Patron service expectations	Checkout process	Cleaning and Janitorial
Helen Young	General Manager	✓				✓	✓		✓	✓	
Mitchell Fernandez	Kitchen Manager	✓	✓	✓	✓	✓					
Ray Spears	Dining Room Manager						✓	✓	✓	✓	
Lauren Yee	Cleaning Crew Manager										✓

Describe Your Dining Area, Patron Amenities and Service Type

Understanding basic information about your patron experience is needed to determine if specific controls are appropriate to ensure the safety of your patrons throughout their dining experience. Information on factors that increase or decrease the likelihood face to face interactions, as well as identifying any factors that may be difficult to control are important to addressing and minimizing risks to patrons and staff as the plan is developed.

The C-19 Team should capture at least the following information:

I. What is the square footage of your indoor dining area?

II. What is the square footage of your outdoor dining area?

III. Describe your dining room surfaces:
- A. Tabletops
- B. Table linens, if used
- C. Seating
- D. Floors
- E. Walls
- F. Partitions/Dividers

IV. Describe your air flow
- A. Windows – openable or fixed
- B. Air Handling – dedicated to your space or shared with other spaces
- C. Air Filtration – MERV Rating >13, MERV Rating 13+

V. Describe your patron amenities
- A. Restroom facilities – single or multiple occupant?
- B. Hand washing facilities – hand operated or hands free?
- C. Hand drying equipment – air blower, paper towel, other?
- D. Attended or Unattended?
- E. Inspection and cleaning frequency?
- F. Additional patron amenities – VIP lounge, bottle service rooms, etc.
- G. Additional areas that patrons have access to – retail space, hallways, etc.

VI. Describe your service type
- A. Centralized Service
  1. Counter Service – Patrons order at a central location (cashier, self-serve kiosk) and pick up their order at a central location when it is ready.

B. Mixed Service

    1. Patrons order at a central location and their order is brought to the table.

    2. Table service for food, Central service for drinks (i.e. pick up drinks from the bar, use common soda fountain, etc.)

    3. Order from an app on the patron's phone, pick up from a central location

    4. Order from a tableside tablet, and their order is brought to the table

C. Individual Service

    1. Table Service – Patrons orders at their table and their order is brought to the table.

Dining and Patron Area Description

Indoor Dining Area (sq ft)	450 sq ft (Seating for 8 at the counter, Seating for 16 at 4 booths)	
Outdoor Dining Area (sq ft)	200 sq ft (Seating for 12 at 3 tables)	
Indoor Dining Area Surfaces	Tabletops	Laminate with vinyl molding
	Table Linens	Paper placemats and napkins
	Seating	Wooden frame with vinyl seat cushion
	Floors	Sheet vinyl
	Walls	Vinyl wallpaper
	Partitions	Booth height 42" (no top partition)
Outdoor Dining Area Surfaces	Tabletops	Powder coated aluminum
	Table Linens	Polyester napkin
	Seating	Powder coated aluminum
	Floors	Concrete
	Walls	Wrought iron railing
	Partitions	n/a
Air Flow	Windows	2 fully openable windows at front of dining room
	HVAC System	Central heating only. No AC
	Air Filtration	FPR 4 Basic Filter
Patron Amenities	Restrooms	Men's – 2 toilets Women's – 2 toilets
	Hand Washing	Men's – 1 hand wash sinks Women's – 1 hand wash sinks
	Hand Drying	Both – hand operated hot air blower
	Monitoring Frequency	Checked hourly, cleaned and re-stocked as needed
	Additional Patron Areas	Waiting area at host stand – bench with vinyl cushion
Describe Service Type	Standard table service – Individual Service - Host stand - Server - Busser	

Describe Your Kitchen/Back of the House

Just like the patron areas may have issues that require control measures for health and safety, your kitchen and back of the house areas may need steps to be taken to keep your staff healthy. Capturing some basic information about your staff areas will ensure that in the subsequent steps of creating and verifying your traffic flow diagrams will be able to more fully identify areas where staff are likely to have face-to-face encounters with coworkers or customers, high traffic corridors, and high touch surfaces.

The C-19 Team should capture at least the following information:

I.   List of all back of the house areas, with a brief description
    A.   Walk in coolers / freezers
    B.   Dry good storage room
    C.   Linen / paper goods storage
    D.   Produce washing/preparation
    E.   Food Preparation
    F.   Cooking areas
    G.   Drink station
    H.   Expedite counter
    I.   Laundry area
    J.   Janitorial closet
    K.   Bussers' station
    L.   Dish pit
    M.   Employee break room
    N.   Employee restrooms
    O.   Additional area as applicable - receiving dock. alley, trash room, etc.

II.   For each area, identify if it is an enclosed area or open floor plan area

III.   For each area, identify if it is an all staff area or limited staff area. For limited staff area, indicate who has access to this area

Kitchen and Staff Area Description

Area	Brief Description	Floorplan	Staff Access
Walk in coolers / freezers	None – only a reach in	Closed	All Staff
Dry good storage room	Storage closet	Closed	All Staff
Linen / paper goods storage	Storage closet	Closed	All Staff
Produce washing/preparation	Prep sink, table with cutting boards	Open	All Staff
Food Preparation	Prep counter	Open	All Staff
Cooking areas	6 burners, 1 deep fryer, salamander, grill top	Open	All Staff
Drink station	Soda fountain and ice maker	Open	All Staff
Expedite counter	Pick up counter next to cash register	Open	All Staff
Laundry area	Clean towels stored in storage closet. Dirty towels collected in laundry hamper in Janitorial closet	Closed	All Staff
Janitorial closet	6' x 10' janitorial closet with mop sink	Closed	All Staff
Bussers' station	Bus station cabinet with trashcan	Open	All Staff
Dish pit	3 compartment sink Countertop dishwasher with sanitizer rinse 2 drain boards	Closed	All Staff
Employee break room	6 x 8 Room with lockers for employee personal items, time clock, card table and folding chair for employees to use on breaks	Closed	All Staff
Employee restrooms	Single occupancy restroom with toilet and handwash sink only	Closed	All Staff

Create Front of House and Back of House Traffic Flow Diagrams

This is one of the most important steps in developing your site-specific C-19 plan. It is highly recommended to allow for at least an hour for this step.

To create the traffic flow diagrams, the C-19 team will map the movements of patrons and different staff members during a typical work shift. This will help us in future steps to understand where face-to-face interactions are most likely to happen, as well as to understand where our high traffic zones and high contact surfaces are.

To begin, your team will need a scale drawing of your restaurant layout. This can be created by hand or with the use of a drawing app. There are many free or low-cost apps available for iPad, tablet or computer – but a hand drawing is just as functional.

Next, you will need to create a traffic layer for each role (Patron, Cook, Busser, Server, Dishwasher, Etc.). While it is not absolutely necessary to have separate layers for each role, it will make it future steps easier. If you are creating your traffic flow diagrams using an app, layering may require a higher-level subscription. You might also look into creating your diagram using one app and then creating your layers in a second one. If you are hand-drawing your layout and traffic flow, transparency sheets and wet-erase markers available from any office supply store can be used.

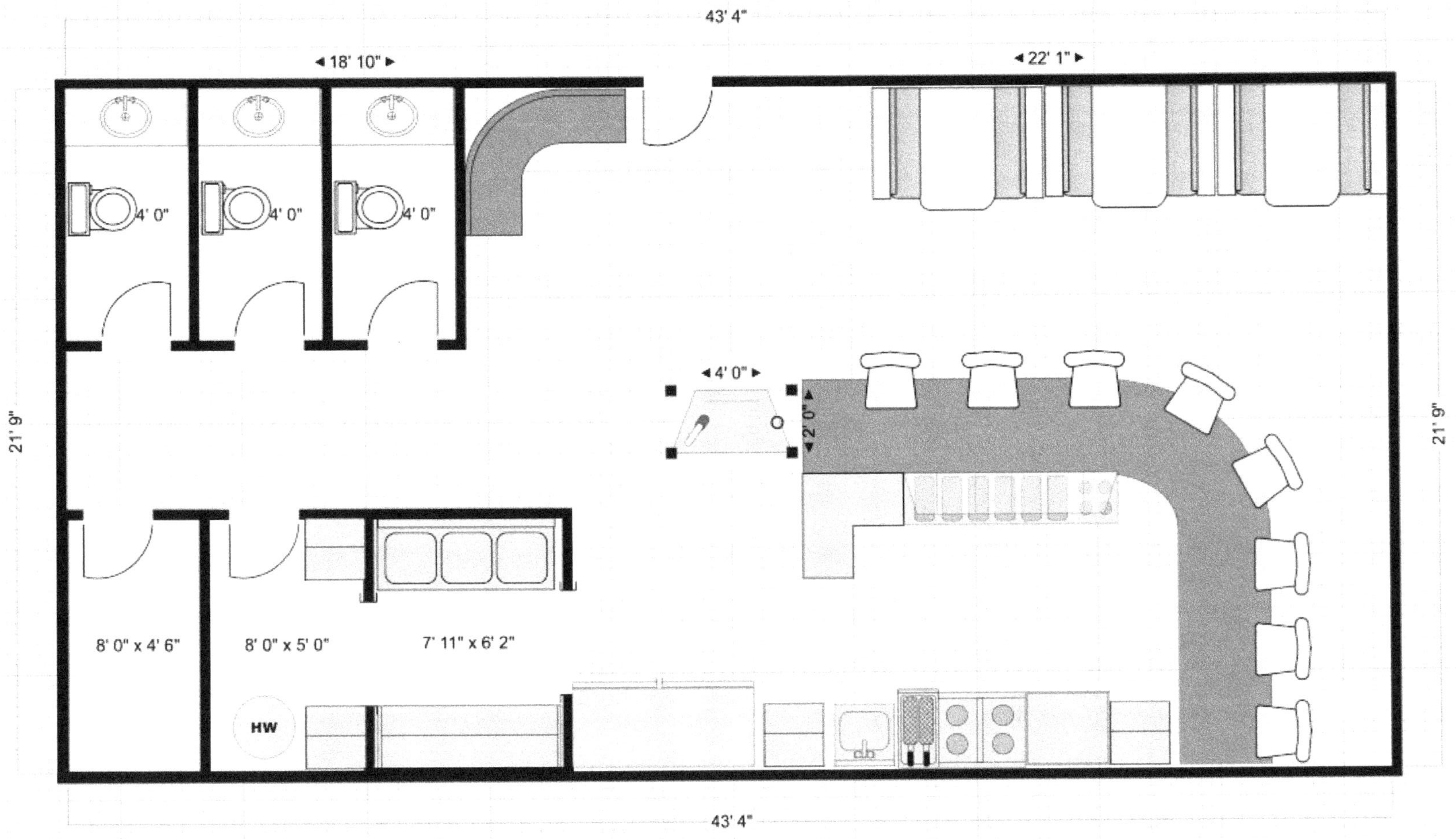

Figure 1 - Basic Diner Layout - created with SmartDraw app

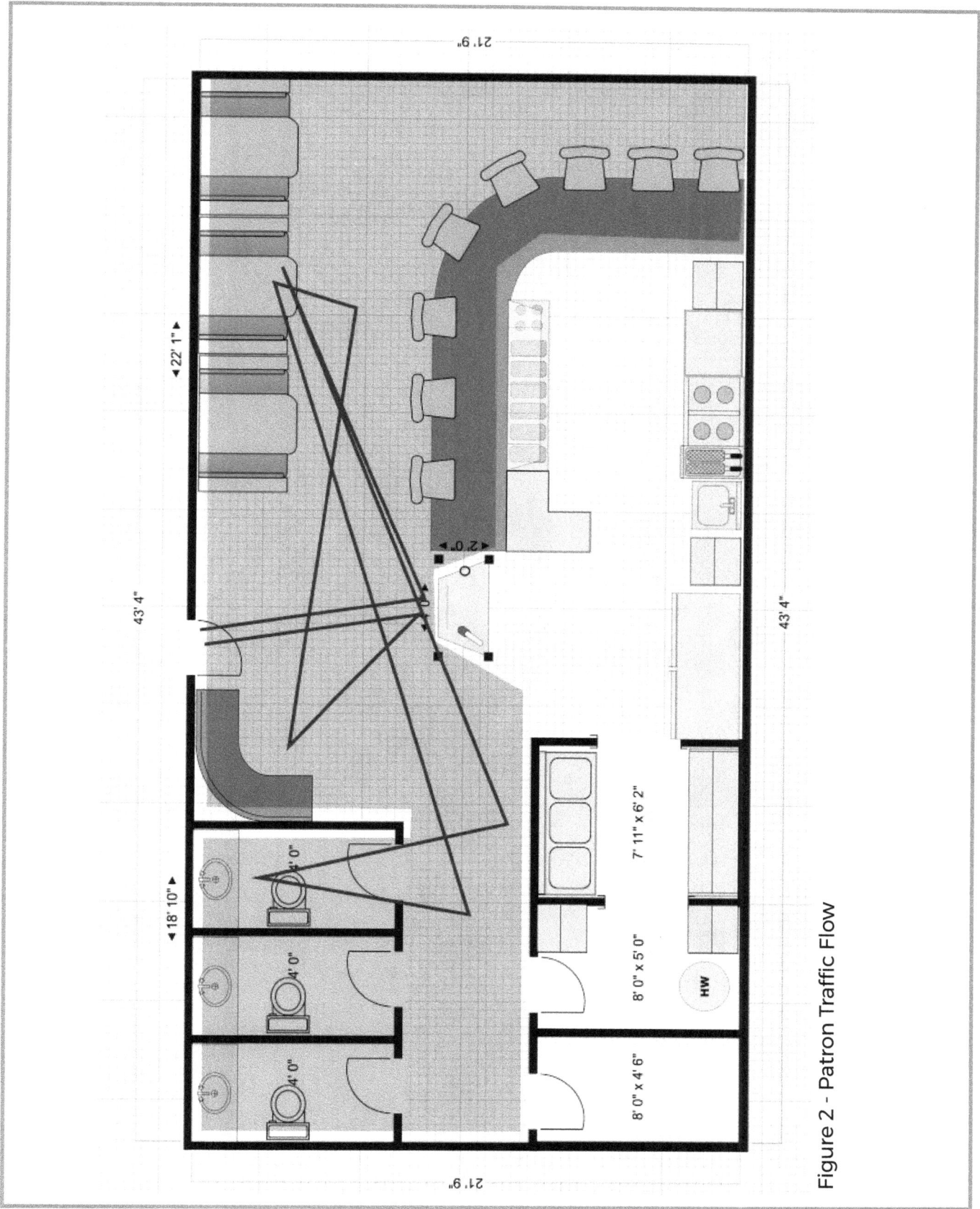

Figure 2 - Patron Traffic Flow

21' 9"

22' 1"

43' 4"

43' 4"

18' 10"

2' 0"

4' 0"

4' 0"

4' 0"

7' 11" x 6' 2"

8' 0" x 5' 0"

8' 0" x 4' 6"

HW

21' 9"

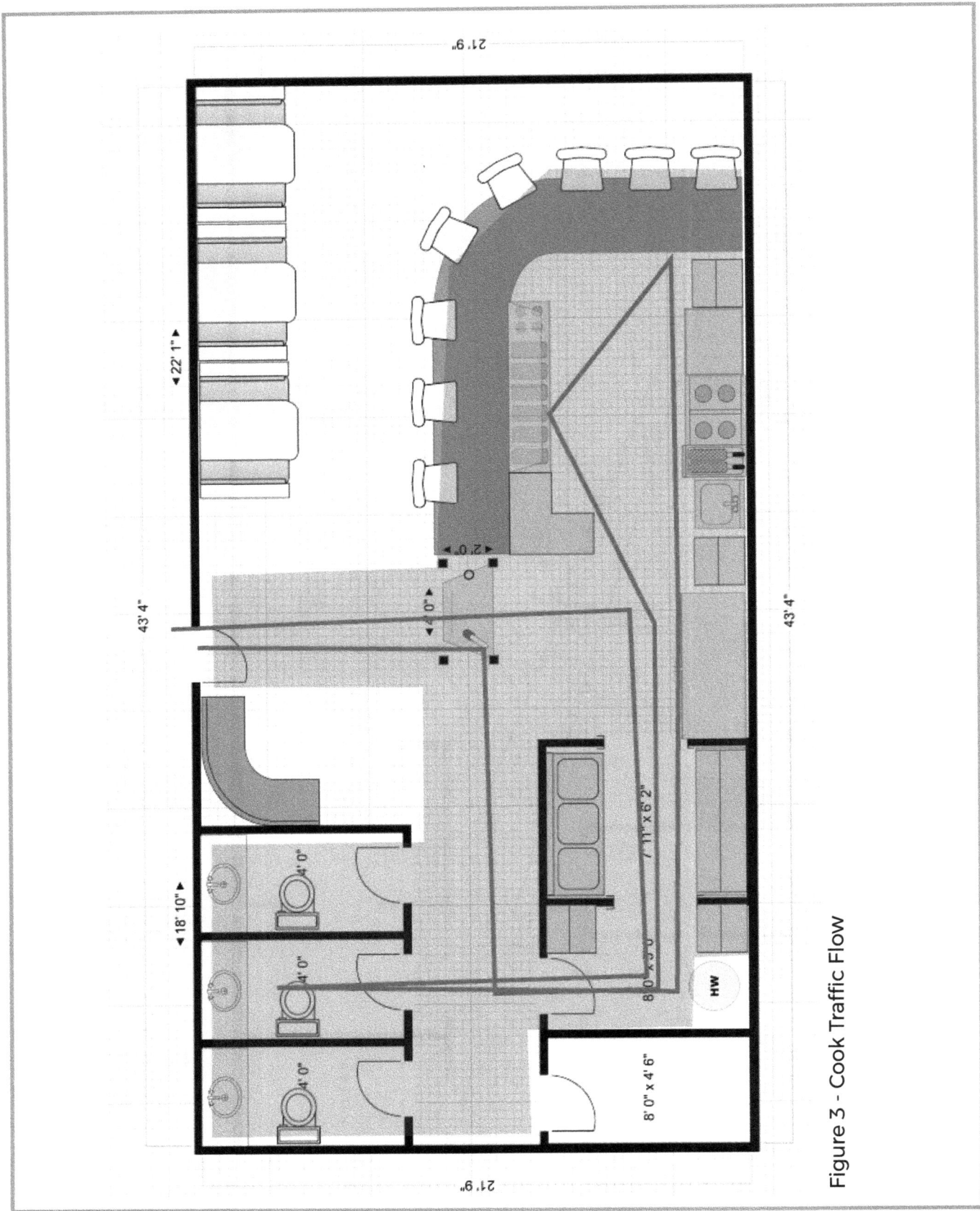

Figure 3 - Cook Traffic Flow

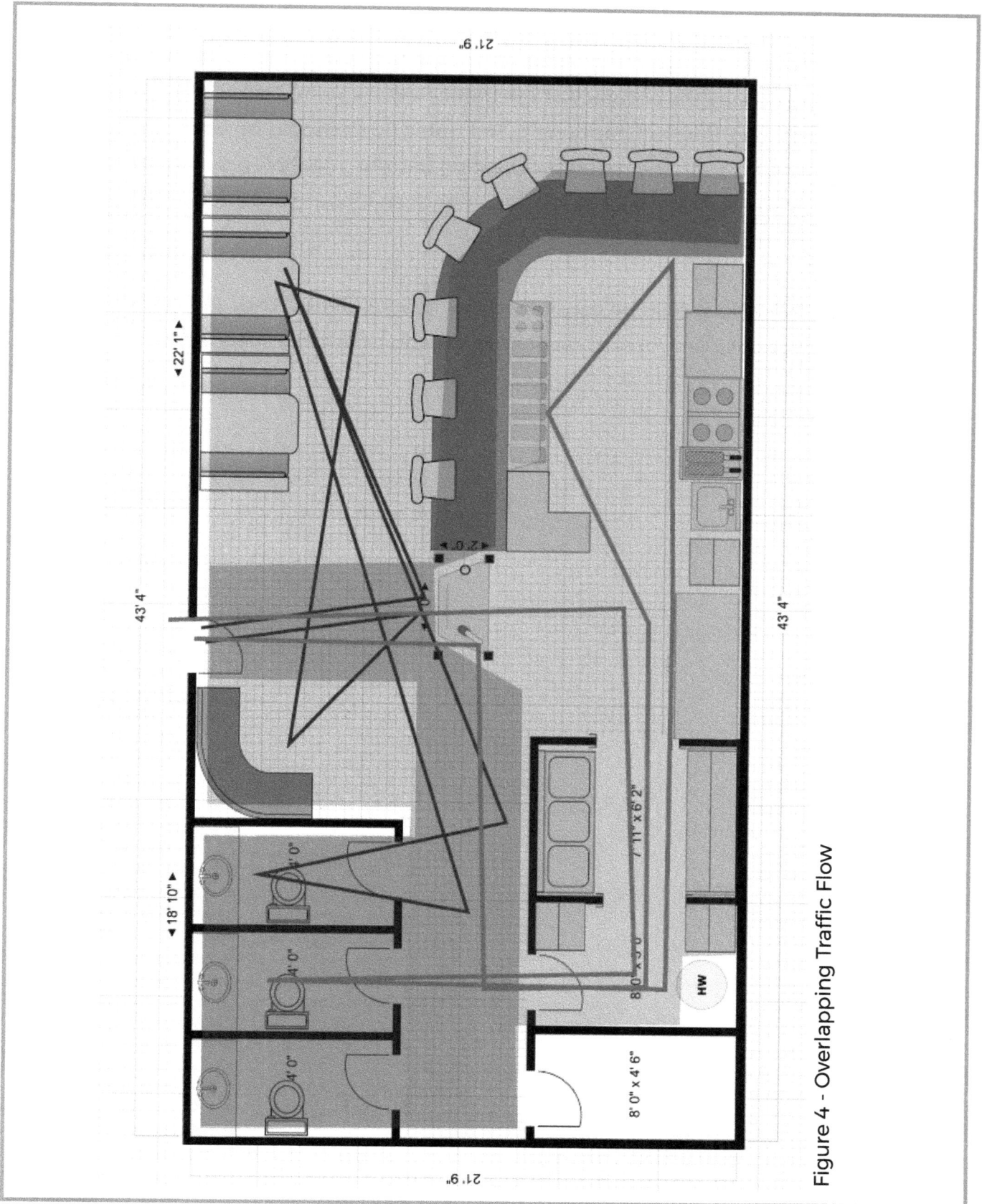

Figure 4 - Overlapping Traffic Flow

45

Verify Flow Diagrams

The C-19 Team must verify the accuracy of the traffic flow diagrams to make sure what they think is happening, is in fact happening. The traffic flows should be physically walked through, even going through the motions of seating patrons, meal prep, service, bussing, etc. This is critical to ensuring that majority of interaction scenarios are captured in the traffic flow diagrams.

The traffic flow diagrams should be considered "living documents." They should be reviewed periodically throughout the C-19 suppression period and updated as needed.

Understand and Control Higher Risk Scenarios

Conduct Risk Assessment

The next step is to analyze the interaction scenarios that each person typically goes through while onsite using your traffic flow diagrams. The team will label the type and average duration of each interaction.

There are 5 main types of interactions:

Customer to Customer (CC) – Face-to-Face between two or more customers from different households and other scenarios where customers may come within 6' of one another

Customer to Staff (CS) – Face-to-Face between customers and staff and other scenarios where staff and customers are within 6' of one another

Staff to Staff (SS) – Staff interactions, including working side-by-side, where staff members are within 6' of one another

High Traffic / High Touch (HT) – These are interactions that do not happen face to face, but individuals pass through common spaces within minutes of one another (greater than 2 people per hour) or touch a common surface before it has been cleaned and sanitized.

Low Traffic / Low Touch (LT) – These are interactions that do not happen face to face. Fewer than 2 people per hour passing through common spaces. Shared surfaces are only touched after being cleaned and sanitized.

There are 3 main duration categories:

- Less than 1 minute
- 1-15 minutes
- Greater than 15 minutes / single interaction or cumulative

The likelihood of infection is dependent of the amount of virus a person is exposed to – with intensity and duration of interaction contributing to a greater likelihood of being exposed to an infectious dose. As explained by Dr. Erin Bromage, a Comparative Immunologist and Professor of Biology (specializing in Immunology) at the University of Massachusetts Dartmouth:

> *"Some experts estimate that as few as 1000 SARS-CoV2 infectious viral particles are all that will be needed. Please note, this still needs to be determined experimentally, but we can use that number to demonstrate how infection can occur. Infection could occur, through 1000 infectious viral particles you receive in one breath or from one eye-rub, or 100 viral particles inhaled with each breath over 10 breaths, or 10 viral particles with 100 breaths. Each of these situations can lead to an infection."*

Why 6 feet for physical spacing?

The recommendation for spacing at least 6' between members of different households comes from the study of exhaled droplets. This is not new science, in fact researchers have been investigating the conditions that increase and decrease the distance exhaled droplets can travel for decades to better understand infectious disease spread and to develop protective measures for sensitive populations, such as people living with cystic fibrosis.

It is known in air quality and infectious disease studies that medium sized droplets move farther horizontally but evaporate relatively

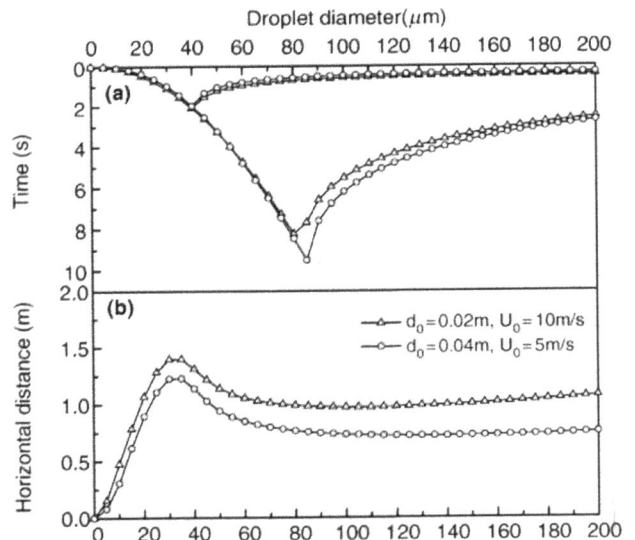

Figure 5 - Predicted behavior of moving droplets of different initial sizes (From "How far droplets can move in indoor environments – revisiting the Wells evaporation–falling curve", Xie et al 2007)

quickly. Larger droplets fall quickly to the ground or a horizontal surface – but take much longer to evaporate. The majority of exhaled droplets, which might carry COVID-19, fall to the earth within 1.5 meters or approximately 6 feet. But, droplets might travel further horizontally if someone is shouting, singing, coughing or sneezing – because they are exhaling with more force.

High Touch/High Traffic Surfaces and Cross Contact

COVID-19 infects people when the virus enters the body through a mucous membrane – usually the eyes, nose, or mouth. This can occur through direct contact – a person coming into contact with exhaled droplets containing virus. This might occur when people are having a close face to face conversation or spending a more extended amount of time in a closed space such as at a choir practice.

Infection can also occur through cross contact. Cross contact occurs when a person interacts with a contaminated surface – like a door handle, and then touches their eyes, nose or mouth before washing their hands. Surfaces can also become contaminated by cross contact – such as when a person with an active COVID-19 infections sneezes or coughs on their hands and then touches a surface before washing their hands.

High-touch surfaces are surfaces that are handled frequently throughout the day by numerous people. These surfaces include doorknobs, sink faucets, chair backs, tabletops, PIN machines and pens. Because these high touch surfaces have many opportunities throughout the day to become contaminated, identifying what and where they are is a key component of understanding the risks to your staff and customers.

Patron Visit Risk Assessment

Interaction	Interaction Type	Interaction Duration	Interaction Frequency
Manually open door	HT	Less than 1 minute	2 times per visit
Speak to host	CS - Host	Less than 1 minute	1 time per visit
Escorted to assigned table	CS - Server	1-15 minutes	1 time per visit
Drink Order	CS - Server	1-15 minutes	1-2 times per visit
Restroom Visit	HT	1-15 minutes	1-2 times per visit
Drinks delivered, food order	CS - Server	1-15 minutes	1-2 times per visit
Food delivered	CS – Server	1-15 minutes	1-2 times per visit
Consume Meal	LT	Greater than 15 minutes	1 time per visit
Check In/ Clear Dishes	CS - Server	1-15 minutes	1-2 times per visit
Dessert Order	CS - Server	1-15 minutes	1-2 times per visit
Dessert delivered	CS - Server	1-15 minutes	1-2 times per visit
Check drop	CS - Server	1-15 minutes	1 time per visit
Change/CC Slip	CS - Server	1-15 minutes	1 time per visit
Sign Credit Card	HT	Less than 1 minute	1 time per visit

Server Risk Assessment

	Interaction Type	Interaction Duration	Interaction Frequency
Manually open door	HT	Less than 1 minute	2 times per shift
Clock In/Out	HT	Less than 1 minute	4 times per shift
Drink order	CS	1-15 minutes	20-30 times per shift
Prep Drinks	HT	1-15 minutes	20-30 times per shift
Drinks delivered, food order	CS	1-15 minutes	20-30 times per shift
Pick Up Food Order	SS	1-15 minutes	20-30 times per shift
Food delivered	CS	1-15 minutes	20-30 times per shift
Check in / Clear dishes	CS	1-15 minutes	20-30 times per shift
Dessert order	CS	1-15 minutes	10-15 times per shift
Prep Dessert	HT	1-15 minutes	10-15 times per shift
Dessert Delivered	CS	1-15 minutes	10-15 times per shift
Prep check	HT	1-15 minutes	20-30 times per shift
Check drop	CS	1-15 minutes	20-30 times per shift

Cook Risk Assessment

Interaction	Interaction Type	Interaction Duration	Interaction Frequency
Manually open door	HT	Less than 1 minute	2 times per shift
Clock In/Out	HT	Less than 1 minute	4 times per shift
Go into walk in	LT	1-15 minutes	8 times per shift
Food Prep Side by Side	SS	Greater than 15 minutes	8 or more times per shift
Prepare plates	HT	1-15 minutes	100+ times per shift
Restroom Visit	HT	1-15 minutes	1-2 times per shift
Kitchen handwashing	HT	1-15 minutes	8 or more times per shift

Identify Highest Risk Activities and Areas

After working through each role's various activities, interactions and movements a picture will start to form of the highest risk activities. These are the activities where there are face to face interactions that take place over a long period of time, either in one interaction or cumulatively over many interactions.

For example – food prep tasks are higher risk for your cook staff because they are required to work side by side in order to do their jobs. Additionally, they must do this for periods longer than 15 minutes throughout their shift.

On the other hand, customer/staff interactions between customers and servers, bussers and your dining room host are all brief interactions but there are several in each patron visit. From a customer risk point of view, they may accumulate greater than 15 minutes of close interactions with staff. But, from a staff risk point of view your front of house staff are having a full shift of those interactions – much greater than 15 minutes of cumulative exposure.

While reviewing the risk assessments for each role, take this time to also review that role's movement through high traffic areas by moving their layer to the top of the traffic flow diagram. This will show you the high traffic areas that impact each role.

Patron Visit Risk Assessment

Interaction	Interaction Type	Interaction Duration	Interaction Frequency	Higher Risk Activities
Manually open door	HT	Less than 1 minute	2 times per visit	Yes – High Touch
Speak to host	CS - Host	Less than 1 minute	1 time per visit	
Escorted to assigned table	CS - Server	1-15 minutes	1 time per visit	Yes - Cumulative
Drink Order	CS - Server	1-15 minutes	1-2 times per visit	Yes - Cumulative
Restroom Visit	HT	1-15 minutes	1-2 times per visit	Yes – High Touch
Drinks delivered, food order	CS - Server	1-15 minutes	1-2 times per visit	Yes - Cumulative
Food delivered	CS – Server	1-15 minutes	1-2 times per visit	Yes - Cumulative
Consume Meal	LT	Greater than 15 minutes	1 time per visit	
Check In/ Clear Dishes	CS - Server	1-15 minutes	1-2 times per visit	Yes - Cumulative
Dessert Order	CS - Server	1-15 minutes	1-2 times per visit	Yes - Cumulative
Dessert delivered	CS - Server	1-15 minutes	1-2 times per visit	Yes - Cumulative
Check drop	CS - Server	1-15 minutes	1 time per visit	Yes - Cumulative
Change/CC Slip	CS - Server	1-15 minutes	1 time per visit	Yes - Cumulative
Sign Credit Card	HT	Less than 1 minute	1 time per visit	Yes – High Touch

Develop Specific Risk Reduction Actions

Reopening for dine-in service will not be without risk. There are certain face to face interactions that are essential to providing service and there are physical constraints to our establishments that will create higher traffic areas. Once we've made the decision to reopen, we must be committed to reducing risks where possible, especially for the highest risk areas and activities.

To reduce risk, we must take steps to:
- Reduce prolonged close interactions
  - Customer to Customer
  - Staff to Staff
  - Customer to Staff
- Reduce prolonged time in high traffic areas
- Frequently break cross contact cycle for high touch surfaces

Some actions to reduce Prolonged Close Customer to Customer Interactions
- Ensure there are clear markings, stanchions or other physical guides to help customers queue following 6 foot spacing
- Ensure that customers are not seated within 6 feet of other parties
- Ensure that queues for the restroom, cashier stand, or other high traffic areas are well organized with clear signage showing where customers should queue

Some actions to reduce Prolonged Close Staff to Staff Interactions
- Work with supply chain to receive pre-chopped vegetables vs processing in-house
- Consider having reduced service hours so some ingredient prep can happen with shift staggering in off hours
- Reduce menu complexity so fewer ingredients are needed to be prepped daily and smaller staff headcount is needed

Some actions to reduce Prolonged Close Customer to Staff Interactions

- Simplify ordering process.
  - Fixed Price Menu
  - Reduced menu complexity – shorter time tableside for servers explaining menu
  - Reduce customizations available
- Take full order at beginning of service. This will potentially reduce the average check amount, but will reduce the number of contacts the server will need to make with the party.
- Use ordering tablets or an ordering kiosk. This creates a high touch surface, but reduces face to face contacts
- Provide face masks for all staff - washable or disposable

Some actions to reduce Prolonged Time in High Traffic Areas

- If possible, have all queueing outdoors. Place plants or stored furniture in open spaces near your host stand where customers may be tempted to queue.
- Convert multi-occupant restrooms to single occupant restrooms and install lights or other indicators that can easily communicate if a restroom is occupied
- Use a staggered reservation system so fewer customers are moving through high traffic areas per hour

Some actions to frequently break cross contact cycle for high touch surfaces

- Provide hand sanitizer stands in all high traffic areas, especially where there are also high touch surfaces such as at the cashier and host stands.
- Place sanitizing supplies close to high touch surfaces to enable staff to quickly sanitize these surfaces before and/or after interacting with them – Sanitizer towels or wipes, alcohol-based sprays, etc.
- Create a general housekeeping position on staff with responsibility to continuously clean and sanitize high touch surfaces.

Excerpt from CDC Guidance

CDC Activities and Initiatives Supporting the COVID-19 Response and the President's Plan for Opening America Up Again - Appendix F

Scaling Up Operations

In all Steps:

- Establish and maintain communication with local and state authorities to determine current mitigation levels in your community.
- Consider assigning workers at high risk for severe illness duties that minimize their contact with customers and other employees (e.g., managing inventory rather than working as a cashier, managing administrative needs through telework).
- Provide employees from higher transmission areas (earlier Step areas) telework and other options as
- feasible to eliminate travel to workplaces in lower transmission (later Step) areas and vice versa.

Step 1: Bars remain closed and restaurant service should remain limited to drive-through, curbside take out, or delivery with strict social distancing.

Step 2: Bars may open with limited capacity; restaurants may open dining rooms with limited seating capacity that allows for social distancing.

Step 3: Bars may open with increased standing room occupancy that allows for social distancing; restaurants may operate while maintaining social distancing.

Promote healthy hygiene practices

- Enforce hand washing, covering coughs and sneezes, and use of a cloth face coverings by employees when near other employees and customers.
- Ensure adequate supplies to support healthy hygiene practices for both employees and customers including soap, hand sanitizer with at least 60 percent alcohol (on every table, if supplies allow), paper towels, and tissues.

- Post signs on how to stop the spread of COVID-19 properly wash hands, promote everyday protective measures, and properly wear a face covering.

Intensify cleaning, disinfection, and ventilation

- Clean and disinfect frequently touched surfaces (for example, door handles, workstations, cash registers) at least daily and shared objects (for example, payment terminals, tables, countertops/bars, receipt trays, condiment holders) between use. Use products that meet EPA's criteria for use against SARS-CoV-2 and that are appropriate for the surface. Prior to wiping the surface, allow the disinfectant to sit for the necessary contact time recommended by the manufacturer. Train staff on proper cleaning procedures to ensure safe and correct application of disinfectants.
- Make available individual disinfectant wipes in bathrooms.
- Wash, rinse, and sanitize food contact surfaces, food preparation surfaces, and beverage equipment after use.
- Avoid using or sharing items such as menus, condiments, and any other food. Instead, use disposable or digital menus, single serving condiments, and no-touch trash cans and doors.
- Use touchless payment options as much as possible, when available. Ask customers and employees to exchange cash or card payments by placing on a receipt tray or on the counter rather than by hand. Clean and disinfect any pens, counters, or hard surfaces between use or customer.
- Use disposable food service items (utensils, dishes). If disposable items are not feasible, ensure that all non-disposable food service items are handled with gloves and washed with dish soap and hot water or in a dishwasher. Employees should wash their hands after removing their gloves or after directly handling used food service items
- Use gloves when removing garbage bags or handling and disposing of trash and wash hands afterwards
- Avoid using food and beverage containers or utensils brought in by customers.
- Ensure that ventilation systems operate properly and increase circulation of outdoor air as much as possible such as by opening windows and doors. Do not open windows and doors if doing so poses a safety risk to employees, children, or customers.
- Take steps to ensure that all water systems and features (for example, drinking fountains, decorative
- fountains) are safe to use after a prolonged facility shutdown to minimize the risk

Best Practices for Re-Opening Retail Food Establishments During the COVID-19 Pandemic

FDA U.S. FOOD & DRUG ADMINISTRATION

We encourage retail food establishments and their employees to follow these best practices and refer to the checklist for more details. Work closely with State and local regulatory/health authorities where the business is located to ensure all requirements are met.

BE HEALTHY, BE CLEAN

Stay home, if sick.

Check for symptoms like fever, cough, difficulty breathing, and consider conducting health checks prior to starting work.

Wash hands often with soap and water for at least 20 seconds.

Don't touch Ready-To-Eat foods with bare hands.

Wear cloth face coverings if Personal Protective Equipment is not required. Check State or local guidelines.

CLEAN & DISINFECT

Clean and disinfect high-touch surfaces and common use areas more frequently, such as door knobs and handles, display cases, check-out counter, order kiosks, grocery cart handles, restrooms, and waiting areas.
Clean and sanitize equipment like ice machines and ice bins.

Prepare and use sanitizers and disinfectants according to label instructions.

Avoid high-touch containers and items like ketchup bottles, utensils, salt/pepper shakers, and reusable menus by using single service items, when possible.

FDA Infographic Best Practices for Reopening Retail Food Establishments During the COVID-19 Pandemic (Page 2)

SOCIAL DISTANCE

Restrict the number of workers, customers and visitors in sit-in dining areas, bars and in shared spaces like kitchens, break rooms, waiting areas, and offices to maintain at least a 6-foot distance between people.

Increase spacing for customers and increase utensil disinfection and cleaning frequency at self-service stations/buffets.

Minimize contact at check-out and pay stations. Mark 6-foot distances with floor tape and temporarily move workstations to create more distance, consider installing partitions, if feasible.

PICK-UP & DELIVERY

Maintain food time and temperature controls.

Initiate "no touch" deliveries and payments.

Designate pick-up zones.

PHYSICAL FACILITY

Ensure premises are operational and in good working order.

Clean, disinfect, and sanitize throughout the facility before re-opening.

Monitor for pests.

Risk Reduction Actions

Interaction	Manually Opening Door
Interaction Type	High Touch (HT)
Higher Risk to Who	Customers and Staff
Risk Reduction Actions	• Leave door open during business hours, weather permitting • Place hand sanitizer stand at entrance • Sanitizer towels stored at host stand, door handles wiped at least hourly at the top of the hour

Develop Plan Monitoring System

After taking the time and effort to create this plan, it is important to make sure that it is put into action on a daily basis. You may be tempted to skip over creating a formal monitoring system for your C-19 plan, thinking that with the heightened awareness around this seriousness of the virus your full staff will be focused on making sure the plan is in action. This may be true for the first weeks of reopening, but it is unlikely to continue without specific assigned responsibilities.

Monitoring of your C-19 plan is a planned sequence of specific checks to assess whether your plan is operating as intended. The purpose of doing monitoring as a planned check is to ensure that throughout the day the plan is working, no matter how busy or stressful the day is.

Elements of the monitoring system

How you monitor your plan depends on the specific risk reduction actions that you chose in the previous step, but they can be outlined as follows:

What needs to be checked?
- How is it checked?
- How often does it need to be checked?
- Who will check?

It is important that there are staff members with the specific responsibility to check that the plan is in action, according to the monitoring schedule that the C-19 team establishes. Additionally, this ensures that staff members receive any training necessary to effectively perform monitoring checks, such as how to check sanitizer concentration.

Interaction	Manually Opening Door
Interaction Type	High Touch (HT)
Higher Risk to Who	Customers and Staff
Risk Reduction Actions	• Leave door open during business hours, weather permitting • Place hand sanitizer stand at entrance • Sanitizer towels stored at host stand, door handles wiped at least hourly at the top of the hour
What needs to be checked?	• Check to make sure door is open • Check to make sure sanitizer stand is in place and stocked • Check to make sure sanitizer towels are at host stand • Confirm sanitizer ppm in the red bucket • Confirm with staff that door handles were wiped at the top of the hour
How is it checked?	Checks are done visually and verbally
How often does it need to be checked?	Hourly – at quarter past the hour
Who will check?	Front end manager on duty

Develop Plan Enforcement Procedures

When monitoring or other observations identify that the plan is not working as intended it is important to enforce the plan for the health and safety of patrons and staff. Oftentimes a simple reminder is all that is needed to put the plan back on track. Other times, however more forceful enforcement might be needed and it is important to have a plan of how those incidents should be handled to make it easier for your staff to resolve issues as quickly as possible. Established enforcement procedures tell staff that the C-19 team has thought through likely challenges that they might face with enforcing the plan with one another and with patrons, and that there is a defined approach that should be taken. This takes the guess work out of potentially tense situations.

It can be helpful to create an enforcement quick chart to help staff know when they should involve managers or other senior staff to help them enforce the C-19 plan.

Enforcement Procedure

Scenario	Customers not observing 6 ft spacing in the queue
1ˢᵗ Response	Gentle reminder: 'Hi, thank you for joining us today. Please sure your party stays at the mark to ensure we have 6 ft spacing for everyone's safety"
2ⁿᵈ Response	Firm Reminder: "Please make sure you are observing 6 ft spacing, or we will not be able to hold your spot in the line for dine-in service."
3ʳᵈ Response	If the customer still does not follow the spacing guide on the sidewalk, notify the front-end manager on duty. They will: 1. Notify the customer that they have lost their space for dine in service and be offered take out service. 2. If they choose take out service, they will be asked to wait in their car
4ᵗʰ Response	If the customer further escalates, the front-end manager will attempt to guide them away from the front of the restaurant and attempt to diffuse the situation at a safer distance from other staff and customers. The customer will not be permitted to dine-in that day.

(4)

Implement Your COVID-19 Prevention Plan

Preparing Your Staff

Training – Leading Change in Actions and Processes

An integral part of reopening safely for employees and customers is through communication and training. Due to the complexity of the COVID-19 virus there is an increase of touch points that both managers and employees need to understand and know how to respond too.

Empathy and transparency will go a long way with employees as they return to work. Flexibility is recommended for employees to adapt to new stricter policies and procedures. They may need more time to get to work, to setup their workspace, and answer customer's questions. Checking-in daily with employees builds trust and understanding, especially if they may have concerns for their personal safety and those around them. Training assists with getting everyone to work together.

Develop the Training Program

The first step is to involve the additional memebers of the management team to ensure that everyone is on board with what actions need to be completed to re-open and who will be responsible for each task. The full management team will need to work together to provide employee training that the staff understands and is able to follow.

Create the Tools and Training Process
- Create checklists to ensure all key points of training are communicated and understood by employees
- Create a Frequently Ask Questions (FAQ) document
- Develop method for monitoring and ensuring adherence to safety and sanitation requirements for employees
- Use Acknowledgement of Training Signature Form to document training

Sample Training Checklist

Pre-Opening

- ☐ Changes to dining and service areas
- ☐ Pre-Reopening cleaning and sanitation of workplace
- ☐ Revised hours of operation, menus, & workplace configuration
- ☐ Continual hand washing and use of hand sanitizer throughout shift and after each task
- ☐ Gloves changed at regular intervals and as necessary after contact with potentially contaminated surfaces
- ☐ Daily sanitation and cleaning requirements for all areas of business

Daily Temperature and Health Screenings

- ☐ Why and how program is administered
- ☐ Commitment to privacy
- ☐ What if employee is ill or been around someone who may be ill
- ☐ Policy for refusal to take test

Changes to Uniforms & Personal Storage

- ☐ Emphasis on personal hygiene
- ☐ No physical contact. No handshakes, hugs, high fives, or fist bumps
- ☐ Wearing facemasks and gloves
- ☐ Company provided PPE
- ☐ Personal cell phone use and sanitation

Changes to Daily Operations

- ☐ Staff meals will not be self serve and to be eaten in an area with social distancing
- ☐ Continuous cleaning
  - Continual cleaning and sanitation of restrooms and other public access areas
  - Sanitation between customers
  - Stocking supplies
  - Frequent sanitizing of high touch point areas (door handles, telephones, workstatons, keyboards, shared equipment, point of sale (POS)

☐ End of day closure procedures
  · Changes for front of house
  · Changes for back of house
  · Food storage
  · Dining and service areas disinfecting and sanitizing
  · Trash removal
  · Handling and storage of used linens, aprons, and uniforms
☐ Cash handling procedures
  · Designated cash handlers
  · Hand washing required after any cash handling
  · Encourage cashless payments

Changes to Dining Areas

☐ Limits to number of customers at a table – no more than 6, must be in the same party

☐ New floor diagram and table setup

☐ Counter/Bar service partitions between customer, cashier and bartender

☐ Counter service streamlined order process

☐ Every effort made to minimize close contact when serving and clearing tables

☐ Contactless menu such as digital or use of menu boards

☐ Paper menus disposed of after single use

☐ Removal of buffets, self serve beverages, and condiment bars

☐ Pre-packed and single serve condiments only

☐ Changes to table set up
  · No condiments, salt, pepper or sugar caddies should be on tables
  · Do not preset tables – everything should be brought once customer is seated
  · Silverware rolled in napkins

☐ Beverage service changes
  · Garnishes (lemons, limes etc) needs to be in covered containers and only placed on plate or in drink by service staff
  · Beverage refills need to be brought in new glass or cup
  · Wine service – avoid touching glass when pouring and only pour first glass

- [ ] Leftovers
  - Assigned server needs to bring to-go containers to table
  - Customer will need to fill them to minimize contact

Communication Strategy for Customer's Public Safety

- [ ] Online reservation and ordering systems
- [ ] Placing orders – online and in-person
- [ ] Upon arrival where to wait for table
- [ ] Methods of payments – especially if going cashless
- [ ] Customer face mask policy
- [ ] Managing questions from customers
- [ ] Review Frequently Asked Questions (FAQ) document
- [ ] Review posted signage

Customer Service Guidelines

- [ ] Reassuring customers that safety and sanitation procedures have been implemented and followed from opening to close is the utmost importance
- [ ] Health check policy for customers
- [ ] Provide disposable masks for customers that do not have one
- [ ] Providing a disposable paper bag for customer to place mask while eating
- [ ] Hands sanitizer and/or wipes available for customers
- [ ] Reservations and priority seating
  - Changes to reservation policy - holding late reservations
  - Communicating health check and face mask policies when reservations are placed
  - Notifying customer that contact information for the entire party will be collected to assist contact tracing if necessary
  - Communicating how to check in when arriving
  - Communicating where to wait
  - How to use the texting software to notify customers that table is ready
- [ ] Collecting contact information, including the names of everyone in their party so that the information can be made available, if necessary, for the Health Department Officials to perform contact and tracing follow up

☐ Data Privacy. Only managers can access contact information. Contact information is deleted after 21 days.

☐ Encourage contactless payment methods

Enforcement Procedures

☐ Review enforcement scenarios

☐ Who can staff bring in to resolve issues with customers?

☐ Who can staff bring in to resolve issues with fellow staff?

☐ What are the consequences for staff for not following social distancing policies?

☐ What should a staff member do if they feel the safety plan is not complete enough?

Basic COVID-19 Training - For All Staff

What is COVID-19 - also known as the Coronavirus Disease?

Coronavirus Disease 2019 (COVID-19) is a respiratory illness that can spread from person to person. The virus that causes the coronavirus is a novel coronavirus that was first identified during an investigation into an outbreak in Wuhan, China.

How does COVID-19 spread?

The virus spreads by droplets made when people with the coronavirus cough, sneeze or talk. These droplets can land in the mouths or noses of people nearby or be inhaled into their lungs. It may be possible that a person can get the coronavirus by touching a surface or object that has the virus on it and then touching their own mouth, nose, or eyes.

What are the symptoms of COVID-19?

People with COVID-19 have had a wide range of symptoms reported – ranging from mild symptoms to severe illness.

Symptoms may appear 2-14 days after exposure to the virus. People with these symptoms may have COVID-19:

- Fever or chills
- Cough
- Shortness of breath or difficulty breathing
- Fatigue
- Muscle or body aches
- Headache
- New loss of taste or smell
- Sore throat
- Congestion or runny nose
- Nausea or vomiting
- Diarrhea

When to Seek Emergency Medical Attention

Look for emergency warning signs* for COVID-19. If someone is showing any of these signs, seek emergency medical care immediately

- Trouble breathing
- Persistent pain or pressure in the chest
- New confusion
- Inability to wake or stay awake
- Bluish lips or face

*This list is not all possible symptoms. Please call your medical provider for any other symptoms that are severe or concerning to you.

Call 911 or call ahead to your local emergency facility: Notify the operator that you are seeking care for someone who has or may have COVID-19.

What steps can we take to prevent COVID-19 spread in our workplace?
- **Stay home if you are sick or have any symptoms associated with COVID-19**

- **Avoid close contact**
  - Remember that some people without symptoms may be able to spread virus.
  - Stay at least 6 feet (about 2 arms' length) from other people.
  - Do not gather in groups.
  - Stay out of crowded places and avoid mass gatherings.
  - Keeping distance from others is especially important for people who are at higher risk of getting very sick.

- **Wash your hands often**
  - Wash your hands often with soap and water for at least 20 seconds especially after you have been in a public place, or after blowing your nose, coughing, or sneezing.
  - If soap and water are not readily available, use a hand sanitizer that contains at least 60% alcohol. Cover all surfaces of your hands and rub them together until they feel dry.
  - Avoid touching your eyes, nose, and mouth with unwashed hands.

- **Cover your mouth and nose when around other people.**
  - You could spread COVID-19 to others even if you do not feel sick.
  - Everyone should wear a cloth face cover when they have to go out in public, for

example to the grocery store or to pick up other necessities.

· Cloth face coverings should not be placed on young children under age 2, anyone who has trouble breathing, or is unconscious, incapacitated or otherwise unable to remove the mask without assistance.

· The cloth face cover is meant to protect other people in case you are infected.

· Do NOT use a facemask meant for a healthcare worker.

· Continue to keep about 6 feet between yourself and others. The cloth face cover is not a substitute for social distancing.

- **Cover coughs and sneezes**

  · If you are in a private setting and do not have on your cloth face covering, remember to always cover your mouth and nose with a tissue when you cough or sneeze or use the inside of your elbow.

  · Throw used tissues in the trash.

  · Immediately wash your hands with soap and water for at least 20 seconds. If soap and water are not readily available, clean your hands with a hand sanitizer that contains at least 60% alcohol.

- **Clean and Sanitize**

  · Clean AND Sanitize frequently touched surfaces daily. This includes tables, doorknobs, light switches, countertops, handles, desks, phones, keyboards, toilets, faucets, and sinks.

  · If surfaces are dirty, clean them. Use detergent or soap and water prior to disinfection.

  · Then, use an approved sanitizer.

What should I do before coming in to work?

- **Monitor Your Health**

  · Be alert for symptoms. Watch for fever, cough, shortness of breath, or other symptoms of COVID-19.

  · Take your temperature if symptoms develop.

  · Don't take your temperature within 30 minutes of exercising or after taking medications that could lower your temperature, like acetaminophen.

- **Complete your pre-shift health screening**

Sample COVID-19 Daily Pre-Shift Health Screening Process

State and public health officials have implemented strict recommendations to control the spread of COVID-19. This includes mandates for pre-shift health screening before work each day. This is a sample form based on standard recommendations for employee Health Screenings and is to provide guidance on how to appropriately screen employees for baseline symptoms related to COVID-19 upon arrival to work, and to continue until further notice from State Health Departments.

Note: Daily Health Screenings do not take the place of other social distancing practices or PPE required in the workplace.

Important Points of Reference on Privacy

- ☐ Before implementing this practice review CDC and local health department guidelines for specific directives for your state and community.
- ☐ If you do not have an HR department – identify who is responsible for overseeing training and answering employee questions. These are sensitive issues and will require good communication skills and understanding of state and local regulations. This includes how to address employees who refuse health screenings without a valid exemption.
- ☐ Provide a "privacy notice" and be transparent to communicate what information is being collected and for what purpose for all employees and managers.
- ☐ Emphasize these health screenings are important to protect the employee's health and those around them. Develop a training program for management based on this information presented.
    - ○ Explain why the pre-shift health screening is being implemented
    - ○ Provide guidance on how to protect employee privacy
    - ○ Proper use of equipment, sanitation, documentation and process for administering the temperature screening
    - ○ How to communicate the policy to employees, potential new hires, and customers

- What to do if an employee is ill, becomes ill, or thinks another co-worker may be ill
- ☐ Identify a location within business where the test can be conducted in privacy.
- ☐ Take strict measures to protect the privacy of the employee and the information collected against unauthorized access or use, including retaining the information for the shortest time necessary.
- ☐ If the temperature or screening indicates potential illness, the individual should leave the premises as discreetly and promptly as possible in efforts to protect their privacy and safety of others.
- ☐ All obligations to disclose an individual's condition for contact tracing should be done with every effort to protect their identity and privacy.
- ☐ Actual temperature readings and health related questions should be promptly removed after daily collection. A business can keep a "pass or no pass" record, yet does increase potential risk to employment privacy laws.
- ☐ Note - the collection of temperature checks and health questions is a temporary partial exemption for personal information that can be asked by employers prior to an employment offer or for re-hiring employees.
- ☐ Employers should remind all employees that it is against the federal law to harass or otherwise discriminate against coworkers based on race, national origin, color, sex, religion, age (40 or over), disability or genetic information. There may be additional protected categories under state and local laws and address workplace harassment related to COVID-19. Advise supervisors and managers of their roles in watching for, stopping, and reporting any harassment or other discrimination. An employer may also make clear that it will immediately review any allegations of harassment or discrimination and take appropriate action. Additionally, employers should review any new anti-discrimination laws relevant to the COVID-19 pandemic specific to their state.
- ☐ Consult with legal counsel for details on additional orders that may apply to your operations.

The health and safety of employees and customers is the utmost of importance for building trust and safety for any reopening plan. Daily Pre-shift screenings is recommended, even if not required for all employees and managers.

Equipment Required

- ☐ Employee Health Screening Form
- ☐ Personal Protective Equipment (PPE)
  - o Face mask covering nose, mouth, and chin
  - o Disposable gloves
  - o Eye protection – goggles or safety glasses
  - o Non- Contact Infrared thermometer or other reliable contactless thermometer

Screening Guidelines

- ☐ Employees are to be paid for all time taken to complete the screening process.
- ☐ Anyone who is feeling sick should not come into the workplace.
- ☐ Temperatures are to be checked in a consistent manner for all employees and managers.
- ☐ Follow manufacturer's instructions for proper use of Non-Contact Infrared Thermometers for taking forehead temperatures.
- ☐ Turn off any sound indicators that may notify others of a potential higher temperature reading.
- ☐ Temperatures should be taken in a private area where other employees cannot see temperatures.
- ☐ Recording of temperatures should be avoided, unless required by law in your geography. All information must be kept in a confidential locked file with limited access and not in an employee's personnel file.
- ☐ Employees can conduct self-temperature checks with authorized equipment and following sanitation and safety guidelines.
- ☐ Employees should be denied entry to the workplace if they refuse screening.
- ☐ Fever is just one symptom of potential COVID-19 illness, additional symptoms are:
  - o Cough
  - o Shortness of breath or difficulty breathing
  - o Chills or shaking with chills
  - o Muscle pain
  - o Headache
  - o Sore throat

Sample COVID-19 Daily Pre-Shift Health Screening Form

Dear Employee,

The health and safety of our employees and customers is our first priority. In response to the recent Coronavirus (COVID -19) outbreak, our company is taking precautions to limit the spread of the virus. Each day all Employees and Managers who enter our workplace must complete the Daily Pre-Shift Health Screening Process. Please review the following self-screening questionnaire upon arrival for your shift:

Have you had close contact with any possible person(s) or at location that someone has been exposed or diagnosed with COVID-19? This includes being within approximately 6 feet (2 meters) of a COVID-19 case for a prolonged period of time; keep in mind close contact can occur while caring for, living with, visiting, working or sharing a room with a COVID-19 positive or suspected individual?

Yes _____ No _____

Have you had a fever of 37.8˚C / 100.4˚F or higher within the past 24 hours?

Yes _____ No _____

Per the CDC, a wide range of symptoms related COVID-19 has been reported. If you have at least TWO of the following symptoms please mark YES:

- Cough
- Shortness of breath or difficulty breathing
- Chills or repeated shaking with chills
- Muscle pain/Body aches
- Headache
- Sore throat
- New Loss of taste or smell

Yes _____ No _____

If you check Yes to any of the questions, please notify management to discuss appropriate guidance.

Please sign below indicating that you have been provided this form and have reviewed the above criteria and do not have symptoms as described. Thank you for your cooperation.

I HAVE REVIEWED THE ABOVE CRITERIA AND DO NOT HAVE SYMPTOMS AS DESCRIBED. I UNDERSTAND THAT SHOULD I FEEL ILL WHILE WORKING THAT I WILL IMMEDIATELY NOTIFY MY SUPERVISOR.

_____   _____
[Print] First and Last Name   Signature:

Date_____

Sample COVID-19 Employee Self- Certification Form to Return to Work

I, _____, attest to the following:

I have had no fever for at least three days without taking medication to reduce fever during that time.

Date of last fever of 100.4 degrees or higher: _____

My respiratory symptoms (cough and shortness of breath) have improved.

Date respiratory symptoms began improving: _____ (write N/A if no symptoms present)

At least ten days have passed since my fever and/or respiratory symptoms began.

Date fever and/or respiratory symptoms began: _____

Employee name: _____

Employee signature: _____

Today's date: _____

Date returned to work: _____

Sample Employee Personal Symptoms and Recovery Form

This form is given to an employee who has developed COVID-19 symptoms or has been diagnosed with COVID-19 and is under home isolation/quarantine. This form is used to monitor symptoms and indicate when they may return to work.

For an employee to return to work them must meet the following three (3) conditions:

1. Employee has had had no fever for at least 72 hours (that is, three full days of no fever without the use of medicine that reduces fevers)
2. Other symptoms have improved (for example, when cough or shortness of breath have improved)
3. At least seven days have passed since symptoms first appeared

This form is for the employee's use only and should not be provided to the employer but kept for the employee's personal records.

Date symptoms began: _____

Date of last fever of 100.4 degrees or higher: _____

Date respiratory symptoms began improving: _____

Date	Temperature	Respiratory Symptoms? (Y/N)	Other symptoms or notes

Sample Employee Training Acknowledgement Form

I acknowledge and have received additional training in food safety and sanitation as it relates to Federal, State and Local Health Department and Company Directives related to avoiding the spread of the COVID19 virus.

Print Employee Name:_____

Signed: _____

Date_____

Manager: _____

Date_____

SAMPLE MANAGERS DAILY OPERATIONS CHECKLIST

Manager & Chef:							
Week Start Date:	Mon	Tues	Wed	Thurs	Fri	Sat	Sun
PRE-OPERATIONS	Y / N	Y/N	Y/N	Y/N	Y/N	Y/N	Y/N
Inspect exterior of building - prepare to address any areas that need attention							
Switch on all equipment							
Verify all cooler temperatures							
Check schedule and confirm staff for day							
Employee storage and break area is cleaned and sanitized							
As employees arrive - conduct temprature and health check							
Review daily log from previous day							
Begin sanitation setup and protocols for pre-opening							
Ensure production logs and recipes have been distributed							
Verify item(s) in Refrigeration and Dry Storage are PROPERLY labeled, covered and stored properly							
Ensure all employees are in proper uniform							
Issure PPE upon arrival							
Associate personal belongings are stored in dedicated area(s).							
Hand washing and hand sanitizer station(s) are properly supplied (soap and towels)and are accessible							
Verify Clean wiping cloths in clean sanitizing solution are present at all workstations. Buckets are available for all stations							
Ensure cutting Boards and utensils are in proper condition							
Verify all food warmer air temperatures							
Thermometers are readily available for all staff							
All areas of the operation are clean and "Inspection Ready"							
Verify all EXPIRATION dates on products							
"READY TO OPEN" (30 minutes prior to opening)	Y/N	Y/N	Y/N	Y/N	Y/N	Y/N	Y/N
Money Bank in the Register Drawer							
POS System test, all works, PAPER in place							
Sanitizer stocked at all workstations and customer access areas							
All tables, chairs and customer contact areas are sanitized							
FOH all product is stocked full and abundant							
All Sneeze Guards and surfaces are dust-free wiped, shiny and sanitized							
Merchandising product present and fresh							
Restrooms are clean, sanitized and stocked							
DURING SERVICE	Y/N	Y/N	Y/N	Y/N	Y/N	Y/N	Y/N
Restroom and workstation hourly sanitizing schedule is followed							
Trash is removed fequently							
All areas of customer contact is sanitized after each seating							
Customers and employees area wearing masks							
Proper glove protocols are being followed avoiding cross contamination							
POST OPERATIONS	Y/N	Y/N	Y/N	Y/N	Y/N	Y/N	Y/N
Entire location is cleaned and sanitized							
Cleaning chemicals are stored in designated areas & properly labeled.							
Verify all food item(s) are PROPERLY labeled, covered and stored							
Verify Hood Filters have been removed and cleaned (DAILY)							
Verify cooking and holding euipment is OFF and pilot lights are On where applicable							
Verify kitchen and servery is clean and all lights are OFF where applicable							
Sanitation/Cleaning List: verify completion of tasks							
Verify that production sheets, and recipes are ready for following day							

Communicate the COVID-19 Prevention Plan to Patrons

Everyone is looking for reassurance as they venture outside for the first time in weeks and months. The majority of the public is eager to get out, yet cautious of being in close proximity of others. So how do you communicate that your company has taken significant steps to make sure that employees and guests feel safe returning to your business?

The answer is multi-faceted. The best approach includes visual cues, signage, a trained service staff that is confident in how to respond to a variety of questions, and a marketing strategy that communicates with people wherever they are.

A few things to consider first:

- Empathy and transparency go a long way. These are emotional and personal times and we are all navigating new ways to communicate.
- Encourage an open dialogue with the management team, employees, local public health officials, vendors and frequent customers to your business. All can assist in crafting messaging that is truthful and sincere.
- Write an FAQ to guide managers and employees on how to answer guest questions even in some uncomfortable situations.
- Plan for push back. Some of the ways of protecting others will require asking people to do things they may not want to do. How you respond sets the tone of how well the requests are received. You will not please everyone and if it risks the safety of others it is okay to say No. Delivering it with kindness will make it easier to accept.
- Be prepared for business looking different for sometime. It is not just about communicating with customers and guests. Regularly check-in with vendors, landlords, bankers and investors to build stronger relationships, allowing for making better business decisions in real time.
- Creativity and innovation are encouraged. Just because everything feels untouchable does not mean it can't be entertaining and may lead to a new service, product, or operating procedure that carries into the future.

The New Dining Experience

Going back to full dining rooms and bars should not happen now. This book is dedicated on how to safely open using outside seating, curbside pickup, take-out, delivery and limiting numbers of people inside. It may look and feel different, but the use of visual cues, a well-trained staff, delicious consistent food and drinks will make it less awkward and more inviting.

Visual Cues

Signage – When and Where to Use
- Entry – marking 6 feet apart
- Where to safely wait to place or pick up an order or while waiting for a table
- Facemask and hand sanitizer requirements to enter
- Any other policies regarding COVID-19
- Cashless payments
- Reservations
- Hours of Operation
- Design – there are a variety of signs available from the CDC, state, and marketing services. If affordable create your own that fit your brand and style

Sanitation and Cleanliness
- Hand sanitizer at entry with signage demonstrates safety
- Hand sanitizer on table indicates commitment to guests and employee safety
- Guests seeing employees sanitizing workstations, POS, and how they clean and reset tables builds trust
- Restrooms need to be extremely clean and well stocked
  - Additional hand sanitizer available
  - New signage with the importance of frequent and correct hand washing techniques for employees and guests

Partitions and Table Blocking
- Select what's best for operation, within budget and aesthetically fits decor
- Be creative – we have seen everything from mannequins to shower curtains

- Plexiglas dividers need to be cleaned and disinfected frequently
  - Choose materials that are durable
  - Expect to have partitions in use for at least 12 months
  - Be sure the surface does not scratch or build up a film when cleaned with disinfectant

Marketing, PR and Social Media

This is the time to tell your story and what actions your company has taken to re-open your business. Develop a marketing plan that includes multiple ways to reach customers. Here are few examples:

- Press Release – Announce reopening date and menus
- Connect with Neighborhood for combined outdoor dining options
- Facemasks – maybe have them custom made with logo or themes
  - Make extras that can be sold with proceeds going to a charity or organization in need
- Logo Hand Sanitizer
  - Individual packets or little containers with logo
  - Partner with other local businesses that may have pivoted to making hand sanitizer, such as breweries or distilleries
- Instagram, Facebook, Twitter
  - Show pictures of employees practicing good sanitation when cleaning, cooking, serving guests or packing orders to go
  - Do a live feed showing how things are prepared
  - Send out special offerings to encourage customers to return
  - Find ways to give back to the community where possible

Going back is not as important as going forward. Developing a clear communication strategy will assist in guiding your company forward as you navigate the future.

Be Ready To Adapt

WASH
YOUR
HANDS

PLEASE
RESPECT
SOCIAL
DISTANCING

5

Sample Documents

3-Month Operating Projections - Based on Limited Menu & Service

	Month 1		Month 2 (30% Increase)		Month 3 (60% Increase)	
Sales		% of Sales				
Food	$72,800	70%	$94,640	70%	$151,424	70%
Beverage	$31,200	30%	$40,560	30%	$64,896	30%
Total Sales	**$104,000**	**100%**	**$135,200**	**100%**	**$216,320**	**100%**
Cost of Sales		%				
Food	$29,120	28%	$37,856	28%	$60,570	28%
Beverage	$18,720	18%	$20,280	15%	$32,448	15%
Total Cost of Sales	**$47,840**	**46%**	**$58,136**	**43%**	**$93,018**	**43%**
GROSS PROFIT	**$56,160**	**54%**	**$77,064**	**57%**	**$123,302**	**57%**
Estimated Expense to Reopen						
Location & Build-out Costs	$5,000					
Marketing & PR	$1,750					
Legal + HR Consulting	$5,000		$5,000		$2,500	
Total RE-open Costs	**$11,750**	**11%**	**$5,000**	**4%**	**$2,500**	**1%**
Operating Costs						
Company Staffing	$56,550	54%	$56,550	42%	$56,550	26%
Marketing & Admin	$2,080	2%	$2,028	2%	$3,245	2%
Operating Supplies	$10,400	10%	$12,168	9%	$19,469	9%
Occupancy Costs	$5,000	5%	$5,000	4%	$5,000	2%
Total Operating Costs	**$74,030**	**71%**	**$75,746**	**56%**	**$84,264**	**39%**
Other (Income) Expense						
Other (Income) Expense	$1,040	1%	$1,352	1%	$2,163	1%
Interest Expense	$0		$0		$0	
Depreciation & Amortizati	$1,040	1%	$1,352	1%	$2,163	1%
Total Other Expense	**$2,080**	**2%**	**$2,704**	**2%**	**$4,326**	**2%**
NET INCOME BEFORE TAXES	**($40,020)**		**($25,314)**		**$1,928**	
Est. PPP - Grants	$25,000		$25,000		$0	
CASH FLOW BEFORE INCOME TAXES	**($15,020)**		**($314)**		**$1,928**	

Sales and Labor Assumptions

ESTIMATE OF AVERAGE CHECK BY MEAL PERIOD *

Based on Estimated Check Average of Limited Menu Offering

	MONDAY	TUESDAY	WEDNESDAY	THURSDAY	FRIDAY	SATURDAY	SUNDAY
BREAKFAST	$9	$9	$9	$9	$9	$9	$9
LUNCH	$11	$11	$11	$11	$11	$11	$11
DINNER	$20	$20	$20	$20	$20	$20	$20

ESTIMATE OF CUSTOMER COUNTS PER DAY OF THE WEEK

	MONDAY	TUESDAY	WEDNESDAY	THURSDAY	FRIDAY	SATURDAY	SUNDAY	
BREAKFAST	50	50	50	50	70	85	85	440
LUNCH	75	75	75	75	90	125	125	640
DINNER	100	100	100	100	125	125	100	750

ESTIMATE OF PROSPECTIVE DAILY SALES

	MONDAY	TUESDAY	WEDNESDAY	THURSDAY	FRIDAY	SATURDAY	SUNDAY	
BREAKFAST	$450	$450	$450	$450	$630	$765	$765	$3,960
LUNCH	$825	$825	$825	$825	$990	$1,375	$1,375	$7,040
DINNER	$2,000	$2,000	$2,000	$2,000	$2,500	$2,500	$2,000	$15,000

TOTAL WEEK SALES	$26,000
TOTAL MONTH SALES	$104,000

Labor Plan

HOURLY STAFF

Position Description	Estimated Daily Start Time	Estimated Daily End Time	Daily Hours - minus break	Wage Rate ($/hr)	Total Daily Wages	Days Per Week	TOTAL WEEK HOURLY
Back of the House							
Utility	8am	4pm	7.5	$10.00	$75.00	7	$525
Utility	2pm	10pm	7.5	$10.00	$75.00	7	$525
Prep	6am	2pm	7.5	$12.00	$90.00	7	$630
Prep	9am	5pm	7.5	$12.00	$90.00	7	$630
Cook	7am	3pm	7.5	$14.00	$105.00	7	$735
Cook	9am	5pm	7.5	$14.00	$105.00	7	$735
Lead Cook	1pm	9pm	7.5	$19.00	$142.50	7	$998
Front of the House							
Busser	7am	3pm	7.5	$10.00	$75.00	7	$525
Busser	1pm	9pm	7.5	$10.00	$75.00	7	$525
Server	7am	3pm	7.5	$10.00	$75.00	7	$525
Server	1pm	9pm	7.5	$10.00	$75.00	7	$525
Lead Server	2pm	10pm	7.5	$15.00	$112.50	7	$788
Host	12pm	8pm	7.5	$12.00	$90.00	7	$630
					$158.00		$8,295

Fringe Rate: 38% $3,152

Total Direct Labor: $ 11,447

SALARIED STAFF

	Wage	TOTAL WEEK SALARY
Chef	$50,000	$962
Manager	$50,000	$962
	$100,000	$1,923
		$769

Fringe Rate: 40%

Total Salary Labor: $2,692

TOTAL PERSONNEL COST: $14,139

$56,558 COST PER MONTH

* fringe rate is benfits cost and payroll taxes

Estimated Expenses for Reopening

	Budget	Actual	+/-
Location Buildout			
Cleaning, PPE Supplies	$2,500		
Materials + Construction	$2,500		
	$5,000		
Marketing + PR			
Printing	$250		
Promotion	$500		
PR	$1,000		
	$1,750		
Legal + HR Consulting			
Legal	$3,500		
Human Resources	$1,500		
	$5,000		
Total	**$11,750**		

Team Leader:
Helen Young – General Manager

Team Members:
Mitchell Fernandez – Kitchen Manager
Ray Spears – Dining Room Manager
Lauren Yee – Cleaning Crew Manager

Team Experience Matrix

		Ingredient Purchasing	Ingredient Receiving	Dry Goods and Refrigerated Ingredient	Ingredient Prep	Kitchen Management	Dining Room Setup	Patron waiting area management	Patron service expectations	Checkout process	Cleaning and Janitorial
Helen Young	General Manager	✓				✓	✓		✓	✓	
Mitchell Fernandez	Kitchen Manager	✓	✓	✓	✓	✓					
Ray Spears	Dining Room Manager						✓	✓	✓	✓	
Lauren Yee	Cleaning Crew Manager										✓

Dining and Patron Area Description

Indoor Dining Area (sq ft)	450 sq ft (Seating for 8 at the counter, Seating for 16 at 4 booths)	
Outdoor Dining Area (sq ft)	200 sq ft (Seating for 12 at 3 tables)	
Indoor Dining Area Surfaces	Tabletops	Laminate with vinyl molding
	Table Linens	Paper placemats and napkins
	Seating	Wooden frame with vinyl seat cushion
	Floors	Sheet vinyl
	Walls	Vinyl wallpaper
	Partitions	Booth height 42" (no top partition)
Outdoor Dining Area Surfaces	Tabletops	Powder coated aluminum
	Table Linens	Polyester napkin
	Seating	Powder coated aluminum
	Floors	Concrete
	Walls	Wrought iron railing
	Partitions	n/a
Air Flow	Windows	2 fully openable windows at front of dining room
	HVAC System	Central heating only. No AC
	Air Filtration	FPR 4 Basic Filter
Patron Amenities	Restrooms	Men's – 2 toilets Women's – 2 toilets
	Hand Washing	Men's – 1 hand wash sinks Women's – 1 hand wash sinks
	Hand Drying	Both – hand operated hot air blower
	Monitoring Frequency	Checked hourly, cleaned and re-stocked as needed
	Additional Patron Areas	Waiting area at host stand – bench with vinyl cushion
Describe Service Type	Standard table service – Individual Service - Host stand - Server - Busser	

Kitchen and Staff Area Description

Area	Brief Description	Floorplan	Staff Access
Walk in coolers / freezers	None – only a reach in	Closed	All Staff
Dry good storage room	Storage closet	Closed	All Staff
Linen / paper goods storage	Storage closet	Closed	All Staff
Produce washing/preparation	Prep sink, table with cutting boards	Open	All Staff
Food Preparation	Prep counter	Open	All Staff
Cooking areas	6 burners, 1 deep fryer, salamander, grill top	Open	All Staff
Drink station	Soda fountain and ice maker	Open	All Staff
Expedite counter	Pick up counter next to cash register	Open	All Staff
Laundry area	Clean towels stored in storage closet. Dirty towels collected in laundry hamper in Janitorial closet	Closed	All Staff
Janitorial closet	6' x 10' janitorial closet with mop sink	Closed	All Staff
Bussers' station	Bus station cabinet with trashcan	Open	All Staff
Dish pit	3 compartment sink Countertop dishwasher with sanitizer rinse 2 drain boards	Closed	All Staff
Employee break room	6 x 8 Room with lockers for employee personal items, time clock, card table and folding chair for employees to use on breaks	Closed	All Staff
Employee restrooms	Single occupancy restroom with toilet and handwash sink only	Closed	All Staff

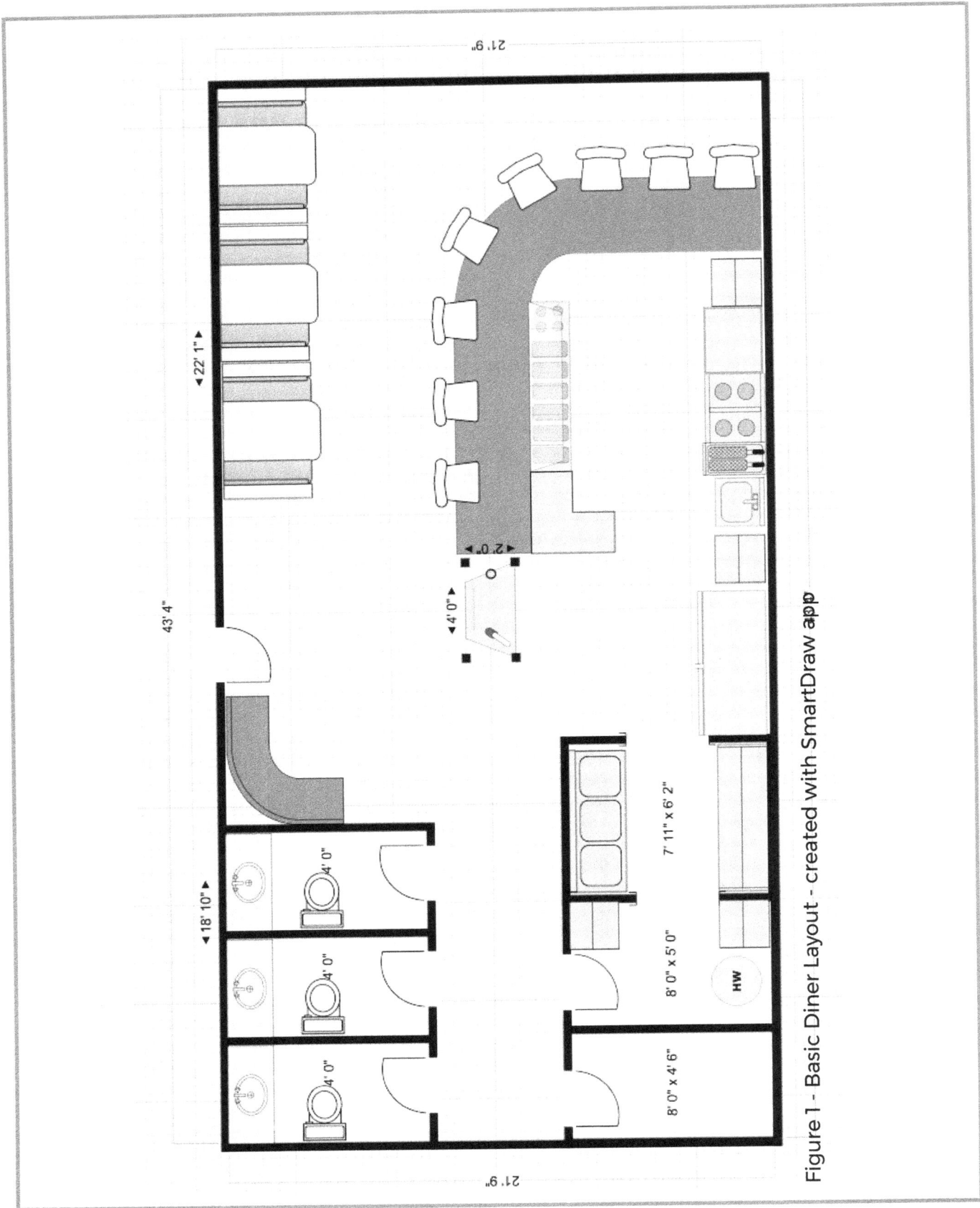

Figure 1 - Basic Diner Layout - created with SmartDraw app

21' 9"

22' 1"

43' 4"

18' 10"

4' 0"

2' 0"

4' 0"

4' 0"

4' 0"

7' 11" x 6' 2"

8' 0" x 5' 0"

8' 0" x 4' 6"

HW

21' 9"

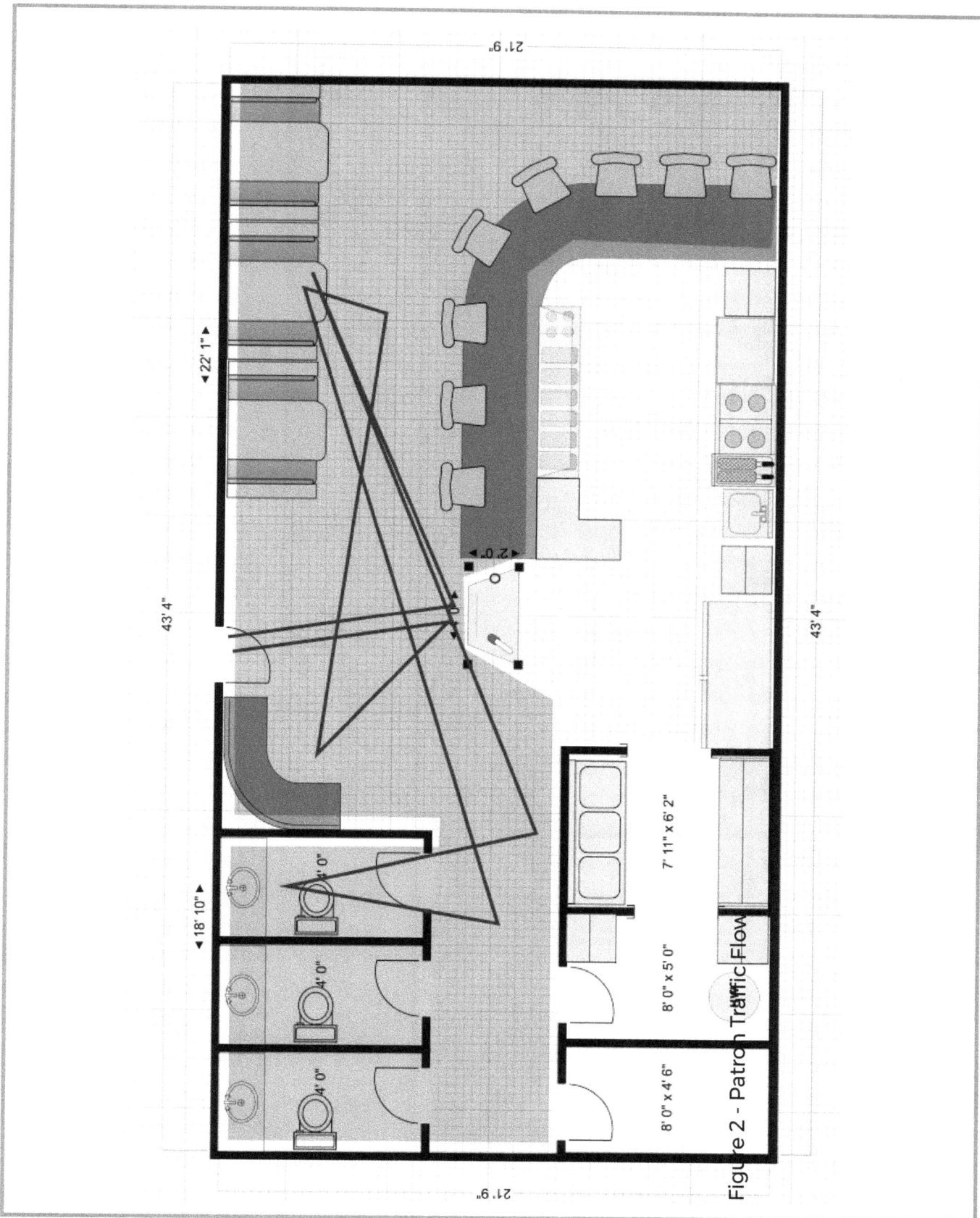

Figure 2 - Patron Traffic Flow

21' 9"

22' 1"

43' 4"

18' 10"

2' 0"

4' 0"

4' 0"

4' 0"

7' 11" x 6' 2"

8' 0" x 5' 0"

8' 0" x 4' 6"

21' 9"

43' 4"

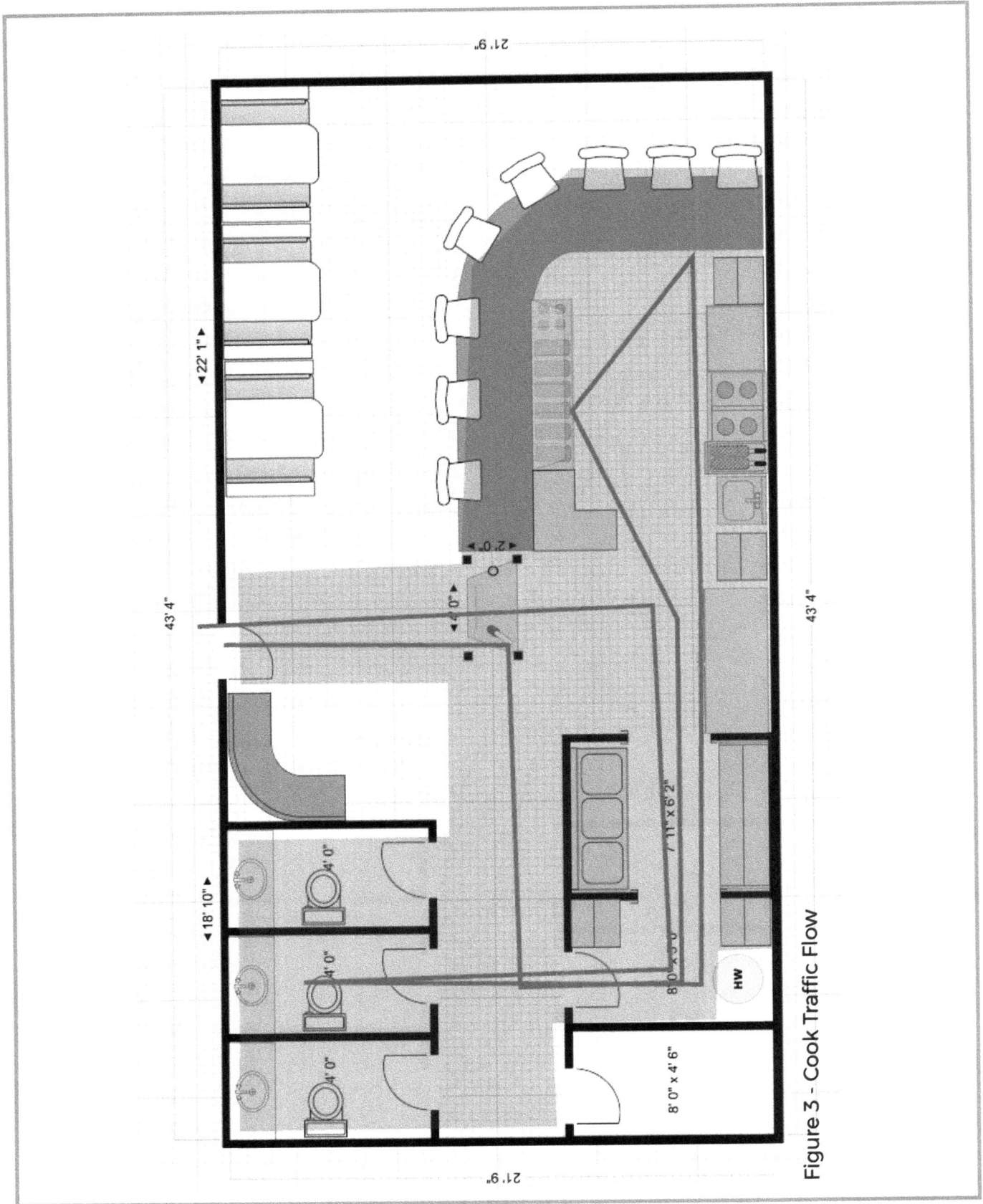

Figure 3 - Cook Traffic Flow

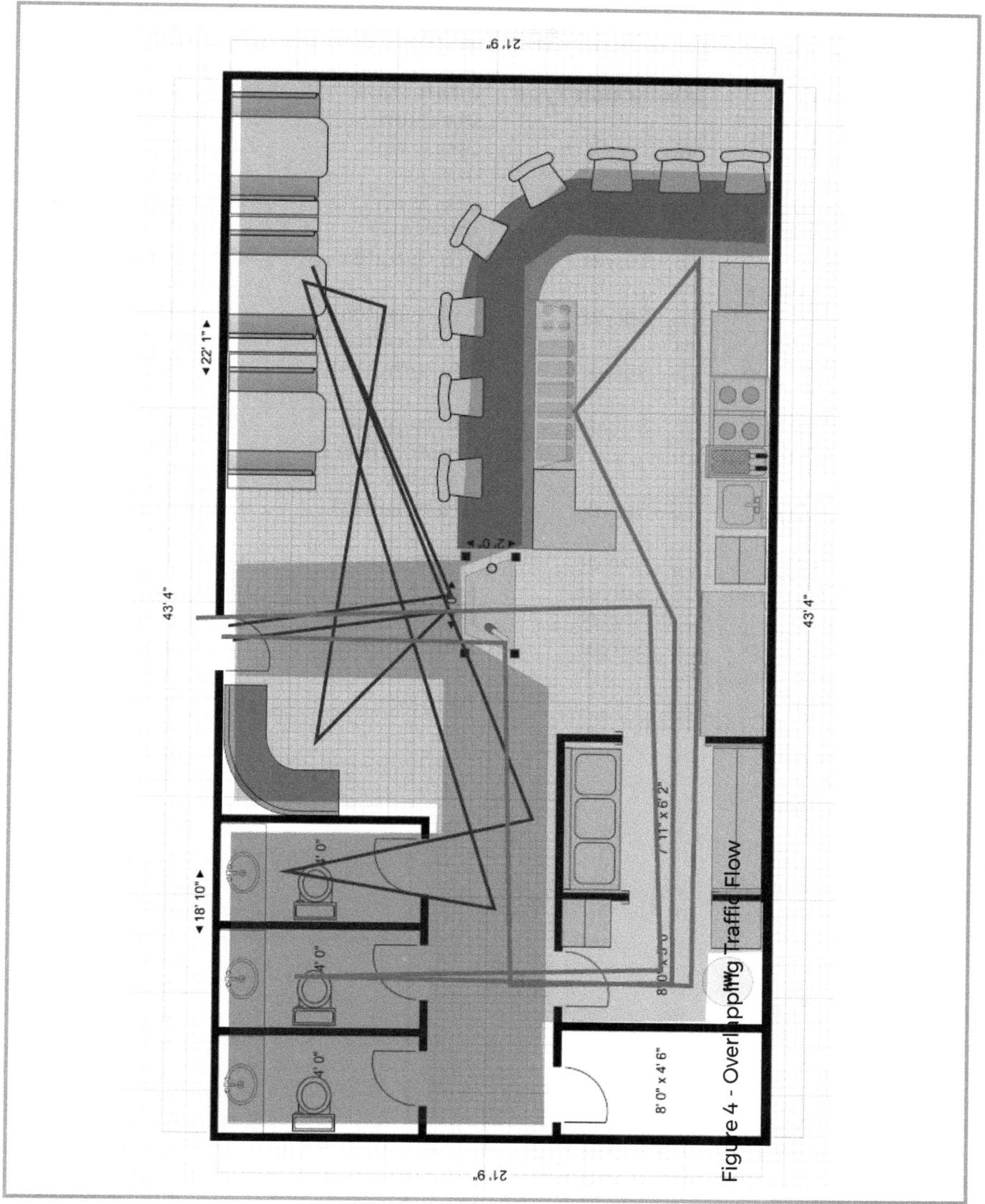

Figure 4 - Overlapping Traffic Flow

21' 9"

22' 1"

43' 4"

18' 10"

43' 4"

21' 9"

2' 0"

4' 0"

4' 0"

4' 0"

7' 11" x 6' 2"

8' 0" x 3' 0"

8' 0" x 4' 6"

Patron Visit Risk Assessment

Interaction	Interaction Type	Interaction Duration	Interaction Frequency
Manually open door	HT	Less than 1 minute	2 times per visit
Speak to host	CS - Host	Less than 1 minute	1 time per visit
Escorted to assigned table	CS - Server	1-15 minutes	1 time per visit
Drink Order	CS - Server	1-15 minutes	1-2 times per visit
Restroom Visit	HT	1-15 minutes	1-2 times per visit
Drinks delivered, food order	CS - Server	1-15 minutes	1-2 times per visit
Food delivered	CS – Server	1-15 minutes	1-2 times per visit
Consume Meal	LT	Greater than 15 minutes	1 time per visit
Check In/ Clear Dishes	CS - Server	1-15 minutes	1-2 times per visit
Dessert Order	CS - Server	1-15 minutes	1-2 times per visit
Dessert delivered	CS - Server	1-15 minutes	1-2 times per visit
Check drop	CS - Server	1-15 minutes	1 time per visit
Change/CC Slip	CS - Server	1-15 minutes	1 time per visit
Sign Credit Card	HT	Less than 1 minute	1 time per visit

Server Risk Assessment

	Interaction Type	Interaction Duration	Interaction Frequency
Manually open door	HT	Less than 1 minute	2 times per shift
Clock In/Out	HT	Less than 1 minute	4 times per shift
Drink order	CS	1-15 minutes	20-30 times per shift
Prep Drinks	HT	1-15 minutes	20-30 times per shift
Drinks delivered, food order	CS	1-15 minutes	20-30 times per shift
Pick Up Food Order	SS	1-15 minutes	20-30 times per shift
Food delivered	CS	1-15 minutes	20-30 times per shift
Check in / Clear dishes	CS	1-15 minutes	20-30 times per shift
Dessert order	CS	1-15 minutes	10-15 times per shift
Prep Dessert	HT	1-15 minutes	10-15 times per shift
Dessert Delivered	CS	1-15 minutes	10-15 times per shift
Prep check	HT	1-15 minutes	20-30 times per shift
Check drop	CS	1-15 minutes	20-30 times per shift

Cook Risk Assessment

Interaction	Interaction Type	Interaction Duration	Interaction Frequency
Manually open door	HT	Less than 1 minute	2 times per shift
Clock In/Out	HT	Less than 1 minute	4 times per shift
Go into walk in	LT	1-15 minutes	8 times per shift
Food Prep Side by Side	SS	Greater than 15 minutes	8 or more times per shift
Prepare plates	HT	1-15 minutes	100+ times per shift
Restroom Visit	HT	1-15 minutes	1-2 times per shift
Kitchen handwashing	HT	1-15 minutes	8 or more times per shift

Patron Visit Risk Assessment

Interaction	Interaction Type	Interaction Duration	Interaction Frequency	Higher Risk Activities
Manually open door	HT	Less than 1 minute	2 times per visit	Yes – High Touch
Speak to host	CS - Host	Less than 1 minute	1 time per visit	
Escorted to assigned table	CS - Server	1-15 minutes	1 time per visit	Yes - Cumulative
Drink Order	CS - Server	1-15 minutes	1-2 times per visit	Yes - Cumulative
Restroom Visit	HT	1-15 minutes	1-2 times per visit	Yes – High Touch
Drinks delivered, food order	CS - Server	1-15 minutes	1-2 times per visit	Yes - Cumulative
Food delivered	CS – Server	1-15 minutes	1-2 times per visit	Yes - Cumulative
Consume Meal	LT	Greater than 15 minutes	1 time per visit	
Check In/ Clear Dishes	CS - Server	1-15 minutes	1-2 times per visit	Yes - Cumulative
Dessert Order	CS - Server	1-15 minutes	1-2 times per visit	Yes - Cumulative
Dessert delivered	CS - Server	1-15 minutes	1-2 times per visit	Yes - Cumulative
Check drop	CS - Server	1-15 minutes	1 time per visit	Yes - Cumulative
Change/CC Slip	CS - Server	1-15 minutes	1 time per visit	Yes - Cumulative
Sign Credit Card	HT	Less than 1 minute	1 time per visit	Yes – High Touch

Interaction	Manually Opening Door
Interaction Type	High Touch (HT)
Higher Risk to Who	Customers and Staff
Risk Reduction Actions	• Leave door open during business hours, weather permitting • Place hand sanitizer stand at entrance • Sanitizer towels stored at host stand, door handles wiped at least hourly at the top of the hour

Monitoring Plan

Interaction	Manually Opening Door
Interaction Type	High Touch (HT)
Higher Risk to Who	Customers and Staff
Risk Reduction Actions	• Leave door open during business hours, weather permitting • Place hand sanitizer stand at entrance • Sanitizer towels stored at host stand, door handles wiped at least hourly at the top of the hour
What needs to be checked?	• Check to make sure door is open • Check to make sure sanitizer stand is in place and stocked • Check to make sure sanitizer towels are at host stand • Confirm sanitizer ppm in the red bucket • Confirm with staff that door handles were wiped at the top of the hour
How is it checked?	Checks are done visually and verbally
How often does it need to be checked?	Hourly – at quarter past the hour
Who will check?	Front end manager on duty

Sample COVID-19 Daily Pre-Shift Health Screening Process

State and public health officials have implemented strict recommendations to control the spread of COVID-19. This includes mandates for pre-shift health screening before work each day. This is a sample form based on standard recommendations for employee Health Screenings and is to provide guidance on how to appropriately screen employees for baseline symptoms related to COVID-19 upon arrival to work, and to continue until further notice from State Health Departments.

Note: Daily Health Screenings do not take the place of other social distancing practices or PPE required in the workplace.

Important Points of Reference on Privacy
- Before implementing this practice review CDC and local health department guidelines for specific directives for your state and community.
- If you do not have an HR department – identify who is responsible for overseeing training and answering employee questions. These are sensitive issues and will require good communication skills and understanding of state and local regulations. This includes how to address employees who refuse health screenings without a valid exemption.
- Provide a "privacy notice" and be transparent to communicate what information is being collected and for what purpose for all employees and managers.
- Emphasize these health screenings are important to protect the employee's health and those around them. Develop a training program for management based on this information presented.
  - Explain why the pre-shift health screening is being implemented
  - Provide guidance on how to protect employee privacy
  - Proper use of equipment, sanitation, documentation and process for administering the temperature screening
  - How to communicate the policy to employees, potential new hires, and customers

- ○ What to do if an employee is ill, becomes ill, or thinks another co-worker may be ill
- ☐ Identify a location within business where the test can be conducted in privacy.
- ☐ Take strict measures to protect the privacy of the employee and the information collected against unauthorized access or use, including retaining the information for the shortest time necessary.
- ☐ If the temperature or screening indicates potential illness, the individual should leave the premises as discreetly and promptly as possible in efforts to protect their privacy and safety of others.
- ☐ All obligations to disclose an individual's condition for contact tracing should be done with every effort to protect their identity and privacy.
- ☐ Actual temperature readings and health related questions should be promptly removed after daily collection. A business can keep a "pass or no pass" record, yet does increase potential risk to employment privacy laws.
- ☐ Note - the collection of temperature checks and health questions is a temporary partial exemption for personal information that can be asked by employers prior to an employment offer or for re-hiring employees.
- ☐ Employers should remind all employees that it is against the federal law to harass or otherwise discriminate against coworkers based on race, national origin, color, sex, religion, age (40 or over), disability or genetic information. There may be additional protected categories under state and local laws and address workplace harassment related to COVID-19. Advise supervisors and managers of their roles in watching for, stopping, and reporting any harassment or other discrimination. An employer may also make clear that it will immediately review any allegations of harassment or discrimination and take appropriate action. Additionally, employers should review any new anti-discrimination laws relevant to the COVID-19 pandemic specific to their state.
- ☐ Consult with legal counsel for details on additional orders that may apply to your operations.

The health and safety of employees and customers is the utmost of importance for building trust and safety for any reopening plan. Daily Pre-shift screenings is recommended, even if not required for all employees and managers.

Equipment Required

- [ ] Employee Health Screening Form
- [ ] Personal Protective Equipment (PPE)
  - o Face mask covering nose, mouth, and chin
  - o Disposable gloves
  - o Eye protection – goggles or safety glasses
  - o Non- Contact Infrared thermometer or other reliable contactless thermometer

Screening Guidelines

- [ ] Employees are to be paid for all time taken to complete the screening process.
- [ ] Anyone who is feeling sick should not come into the workplace.
- [ ] Temperatures are to be checked in a consistent manner for all employees and managers.
- [ ] Follow manufacturer's instructions for proper use of Non-Contact Infrared Thermometers for taking forehead temperatures.
- [ ] Turn off any sound indicators that may notify others of a potential higher temperature reading.
- [ ] Temperatures should be taken in a private area where other employees cannot see temperatures.
- [ ] Recording of temperatures should be avoided, unless required by law in your geography. All information must be kept in a confidential locked file with limited access and not in an employee's personnel file.
- [ ] Employees can conduct self-temperature checks with authorized equipment and following sanitation and safety guidelines.
- [ ] Employees should be denied entry to the workplace if they refuse screening.
- [ ] Fever is just one symptom of potential COVID-19 illness, additional symptoms are:
  - o Cough
  - o Shortness of breath or difficulty breathing
  - o Chills or shaking with chills
  - o Muscle pain
  - o Headache

Sample COVID-19 Daily Pre-Shift Health Screening Form

Dear Employee,

The health and safety of our employees and customers is our first priority. In response to the recent Coronavirus (COVID -19) outbreak, our company is taking precautions to limit the spread of the virus. Each day all Employees and Managers who enter our workplace must complete the Daily Pre-Shift Health Screening Process. Please review the following self-screening questionnaire upon arrival for your shift:

Have you had close contact with any possible person(s) or at location that someone has been exposed or diagnosed with COVID-19? This includes being within approximately 6 feet (2 meters) of a COVID-19 case for a prolonged period of time; keep in mind close contact can occur while caring for, living with, visiting, working or sharing a room with a COVID-19 positive or suspected individual?

Yes _____ No _____

Have you had a fever of 37.8˚C / 100.4˚F or higher within the past 24 hours?

Yes _____ No _____

Per the CDC, a wide range of symptoms related COVID-19 has been reported. If you have at least TWO of the following symptoms please mark YES:

- Cough
- Shortness of breath or difficulty breathing
- Chills or repeated shaking with chills
- Muscle pain/Body aches
- Headache
- Sore throat
- New Loss of taste or smell

Yes _____ No _____

If you check Yes to any of the questions, please notify management to discuss appropriate guidance.

Please sign below indicating that you have been provided this form and have reviewed the above criteria and do not have symptoms as described. Thank you for your cooperation.

I HAVE REVIEWED THE ABOVE CRITERIA AND DO NOT HAVE SYMPTOMS AS DESCRIBED. I UNDERSTAND THAT SHOULD I FEEL ILL WHILE WORKING THAT I WILL IMMEDIATELY NOTIFY MY SUPERVISOR.

_____   _____
[Print] First and Last Name   Signature:

Date_____

Sample COVID-19 Employee Self- Certification Form to Return to Work

I, _____, attest to the following:

I have had no fever for at least three days without taking medication to reduce fever during that time.

Date of last fever of 100.4 degrees or higher: _____

My respiratory symptoms (cough and shortness of breath) have improved.

Date respiratory symptoms began improving: _____ (write N/A if no symptoms present)

At least ten days have passed since my fever and/or respiratory symptoms began.

Date fever and/or respiratory symptoms began: _____

Employee name: _____

Employee signature: _____

Today's date: _____

Date returned to work: _____

Sample Employee Personal Symptoms and Recovery Form

This form is given to an employee who has developed COVID-19 symptoms or has been diagnosed with COVID-19 and is under home isolation/quarantine. This form is used to monitor symptoms and indicate when they may return to work.

For an employee to return to work them must meet the following three (3) conditions:

1. Employee has had had no fever for at least 72 hours (that is, three full days of no fever without the use of medicine that reduces fevers)
2. Other symptoms have improved (for example, when cough or shortness of breath have improved)
3. At least seven days have passed since symptoms first appeared

This form is for the employee's use only and should not be provided to the employer but kept for the employee's personal records.

Date symptoms began: _____

Date of last fever of 100.4 degrees or higher: _____

Date respiratory symptoms began improving: _____

Date	Temperature	Respiratory Symptoms? (Y/N)	Other symptoms or notes

Sample Employee Training Acknowledgement Form

I acknowledge and have received additional training in food safety and sanitation as it relates to Federal, State and Local Health Department and Company Directives related to avoiding the spread of the COVID19 virus.

Print Employee Name:_____

Signed: _____

Date_____

Manager: _____

Date_____

SAMPLE MANAGERS DAILY OPERATIONS CHECKLIST							
Manager & Chef:							
Week Start Date:	Mon	Tues	Wed	Thurs	Fri	Sat	Sun
PRE-OPERATIONS	Y/N	Y/N	Y/N	Y/N	Y/N	Y/N	Y/N
Inspect exterior of building - prepare to address any areas that need attention							
Switch on all equipment							
Verify all cooler temperatures							
Check schedule and confirm staff for day							
Employee storage and break area is cleaned and sanitized							
As employees arrive - conduct temprature and health check							
Review daily log from previous day							
Begin sanitation setup and protocols for pre-opening							
Ensure production logs and recipes have been distributed							
Verify item(s) in Refrigeration and Dry Storage are PROPERLY labeled, covered and stored properly							
Ensure all employees are in proper uniform							
Issure PPE upon arrival							
Associate personal belongings are stored in dedicated area(s).							
Hand washing and hand sanitizer station(s) are properly supplied (soap and towels)and are accessible							
Verify Clean wiping cloths in clean sanitizing solution are present a all workstations. Buckets are available for all stations							
Ensure cutting Boards and utensils are in proper condition							
Verify all food warmer air temperatures							
Thermometers are readily available for all staff							
All areas of the operation are clean and "Inspection Ready"							
Verify all EXPIRATION dates on products							
"READY TO OPEN" (30 minutes prior to opening)	Y/N	Y/N	Y/N	Y/N	Y/N	Y/N	Y/N
Money Bank in the Register Drawer							
POS System test, all works, PAPER in place							
Sanitizer stocked at all workstations and customer access areas							
All tables, chairs and customer contact areas are sanitized							
FOH all product is stocked full and abundant							
All Sneeze Guards and surfaces are dust-free wiped, shiny and sanitized							
Merchandising product present and fresh							
Restrooms are clean, sanitized and stocked							
DURING SERVICE	Y/N	Y/N	Y/N	Y/N	Y/N	Y/N	Y/N
Restroom and workstation hourly sanitizing schedule is followed							
Trash is removed fequently							
All areas of customer contact is sanatized after each seating							
Customers and employees area wearing masks							
Proper glove protocols are being followed avoiding cross contamination							
POST OPERATIONS	Y/N	Y/N	Y/N	Y/N	Y/N	Y/N	Y/N
Entire location is cleaned and sanitized							
Cleaning chemicals are stored in designated areas & properly labeled.							
Verify all food item(s) are PROPERLY labeled, covered and stored							
Verify Hood Filters have been removed and cleaned (DAILY)							
Verify cooking and holding euipment is OFF and pilot lights are On where applicable							
Verify kitchen and servery is clean and all lights are OFF where applicable							
Sanitation/Cleaning List: verify completion of tasks							
Verify that production sheets, and recipes are ready for following day							

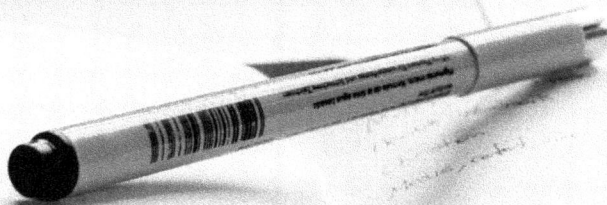

6

Templates

Team Leader:

_____

Team Members:

_____

_____

_____

_____

_____

Team Experience Matrix

	Ingredient Purchasing	Ingredient Receiving	Dry Goods and Refrigerated Ingredient	Ingredient Prep	Kitchen Management	Dining Room Setup	Patron waiting area management	Patron service expectations	Checkout process	Cleaning and Janitorial

Indoor Dining Area (sq ft)		
Outdoor Dining Area (sq ft)		
Indoor Dining Area Surfaces	Tabletops	
	Table Linens	
	Seating	
	Floors	
	Walls	
	Partitions	
Outdoor Dining Area Surfaces	Tabletops	
	Table Linens	
	Seating	
	Floors	
	Walls	
	Partitions	
Air Flow	Windows	
	HVAC System	
	Air Filtration	
Patron Amenities	Restrooms	
	Hand Washing	
	Hand Drying	
	Monitoring Frequency	
	Additional Patron Areas	
Describe Service Type		

Area			
Walk in coolers / freezers			
Dry good storage room			
Linen / paper goods storage			
Produce washing/preparation			
Food Preparation			
Cooking areas			
Drink station			
Expedite counter			
Laundry area			
Janitorial closet			
Bussers' station			
Dish pit			
Employee break room			
Employee restrooms			

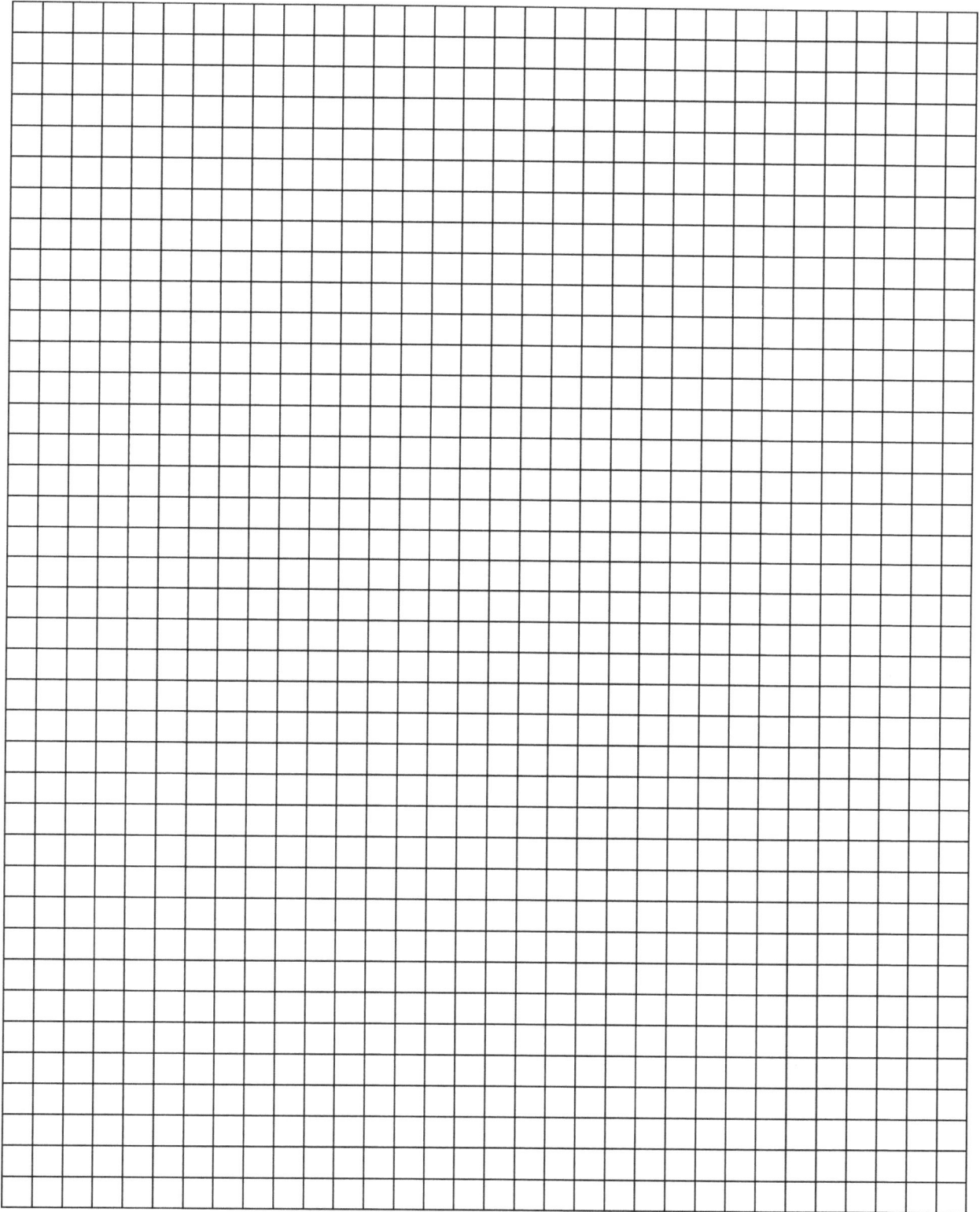

Risk Assessment

Role:_____

Interaction	Interaction Type	Interaction Duration	Interaction Frequency	Higher Risk Activities

Interaction	
Interaction Type	
Higher Risk to Who	
Risk Reduction Actions	
What needs to be checked?	
How is it checked?	
How often does it need to be checked?	
Who will check?	

Scenario	
1st Response	
2nd Response	
3rd Response	
4th Response	

Resources

Human Resources

"5 Questions on Managing COVID-19 and Potential Exposures in the Workplace." Hopkins & Carley, 2020, www.hopkinscarley.com/blog/client-alerts-blogs-updates/corporate-client-alerts/5-questions-on-managing-covid-19-and-potential-exposures-in-the-workplace.

"COVID-19 U.S. Employment Law Update and Guidance for Employers." Insights | Sidley Austin LLP, 2020, www.sidley.com/en/insights/newsupdates/2020/03/covid-19-us-employment-law-update-and-guidance-for-employers.

Official Return to Work Guidelines for Foodservice Establishments . Official Return to Work Guidelines for Foodservice Establishments , National Restaurant Association - Restaurant Law Center, 2020, restaurant.org/downloads/pdfs/business/covid19-return-to-work-guidelines-for-foodservice.pdf.

"Question & Answer Employer Guide: Return to Work in the Time of COVID-19." The National Law Review, 2020, www.natlawreview.com/article/question-answer-employer-guide-return-to-work-time-covid-19.

Marketing

Ruggless, Ron. "Restaurants Unmask Creativity in Protective Gear." Nation's Restaurant News, 26 May 2020, www.nrn.com/workforce/restaurants-unmask-creativity-protective-gear?NL=NRN-01b.

Reopening Guidelines

"Appendix F: Setting Specific Guidance - INTERIM GUIDANCE FOR RESTAURANTS AND BARS." CDC Activities and Initiatives Supporting the COVID-19 Response and the President's Plan for Opening America Up Again, Centers for Disease Control and Prevention, May 2020, pp. 52–56, www.cdc.gov/coronavirus/2019-ncov/downloads/php/CDC-Activities-Initiatives-for-COVID-19-Response.pdf.

Guidance for Retailers and Restaurants to Reopen. Guidance for Retailers and Restaurants to Reopen, Government of the District of Columbia, 2020, coronavirus.dc.gov/sites/

default/files/dc/sites/coronavirus/page_content/attachments/Guidance%20for%20
Restaurants%20to%20Reopen_r6.pdf.

Mancall-Bitel, Nick. "A Guide to All the Restaurant Safety Guides." Eater, Eater, 20 May 2020,
www.eater.com/21265286/restaurant-safety-guidelines-reopening-covid-19-cdc-james-
beard-foundation-food-and-society-program.

General Information About COVID-19

Bromage, Erin. "The Risks - Know Them - Avoid Them." Erin Bromage PhD: 20 May 2020,
www.erinbromage.com/post/the-risks-know-them-avoid-them.

"Interim U.S. Guidance for Risk Assessment and Work Restrictions for Healthcare
Personnel with Potential Exposure to COVID-19." Centers for Disease Control and
Prevention, Centers for Disease Control and Prevention, 19 May 2020, www.cdc.gov/
coronavirus/2019-ncov/hcp/guidance-risk-assesment-hcp.html.

"José Andrés with Dr. Anthony Fauci on Facebook Watch." Facebook Watch, June 2020, www.
facebook.com/chefjoseandres/videos/546591476225102/.

Miscellaneous

Nicas, Mark, and Daniel Best. "A study quantifying the hand-to-face contact rate and its
potential application to predicting respiratory tract infection." Journal of occupational
and environmental hygiene vol. 5,6 (2008): 347-52. doi:10.1080/15459620802003896
www.ncbi.nlm.nih.gov/pmc/articles/PMC7196690/

Xie, X., et al. "How Far Droplets Can Move in Indoor Environments ? Revisiting the Wells
Evaporation?Falling Curve." Indoor Air, vol. 17, no. 3, 2007, pp. 211–225., doi:10.1111/j.1600-
0668.2007.00469.x. onlinelibrary.wiley.com/doi/full/10.1111/j.1600-0668.2007.00469.x

Xie, Xiaojian et al. "Exhaled droplets due to talking and coughing." Journal of the Royal
Society, Interface vol. 6 Suppl 6,Suppl 6 (2009): S703-14. doi:10.1098/rsif.2009.0388.
focus www.ncbi.nlm.nih.gov/pmc/articles/PMC2843952/

This book is dedicated to all the people who work in the food and beverage industry. The work can be arduous, with little profit, yet so rewarding when we come together to break bread, nourish, and celebrate. COVID-19 disrupted our everyday flow and business is no longer how it was. We hope this book relieves some of the challenges of re-opening to establish confidence and trust with employees and guests.

Use this information as a roadmap to develop a program that fits your operation. Look for ways to innovate and build a new culture that can be carried into the future.

If you have questions or are interested in our educational programs contact us at info@mmrspecialtyfoods.com.

We are in this together,

Merril & Rhiannon